Going to Nias

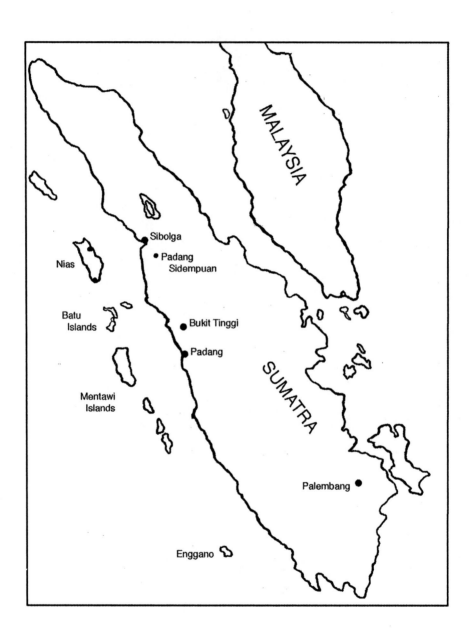

Going to Nias

◆

An Indonesian Adventure

Pat Maximoff

Silamat!

Pat Maximoff

iUniverse, Inc.
New York Lincoln Shanghai

Going to Nias
An Indonesian Adventure

iUniverse books may be ordered through booksellers or by contacting:

iUniverse
2021 Pine Lake Road, Suite 100
Lincoln, NE 68512
www.iuniverse.com
1-800-Authors (1-800-288-4677)

Photographs, Pat and Bob Maximoff
Maps, Bob Maximoff

ISBN-13: 978-0-595-35440-5 (pbk)
ISBN-13: 978-0-595-79935-0 (ebk)
ISBN-10: 0-595-35440-8 (pbk)
ISBN-10: 0-595-79935-3 (ebk)

Printed in the United States of America

For Anna

Contents

List of Illustrations

List of Maps

Preface

I found this letter in an old file. I wrote it in 1956, when Bob and I lived in an oil camp in Indonesia.

At that time, the world was still brushing off the dust of World War II. Europe was digging out. Old colonial empires were cracking or had been crushed by the war.

I was thirty years old when we went to Sumatra, and I thought I knew something of the world. I had toured occupied Germany with the USO. I had worked for the army in Korea when Mao Tse Tung took Shanghai, and I was in Japan when Britain withdrew from India. But I knew next to nothing about Southeast Asia, and I had tucked Indonesia into a mental file of newly independent countries that grew a lot of coffee.

A few trips to the library showed me how wrong I was!

Indonesia is immense! If you put its east end on New York City and spread Indonesia out over the continental United States, the province of Aceh would be several hundreds of miles out in the Pacific Ocean.

Indonesia is an island country, but three of its islands are among the six largest in the world.

Indonesia has the largest Moslem population in the world, but it has sizable numbers of Christians, Buddhists, and Hindus, too. The government has made no attempt to count the number of different ethnic groups. According to *Ethnologue*, Indonesia has 737 living languages; 49 of these are in Sumatra.

Sumatra, alone, is bigger than the state of California, bigger than the country of Japan, and almost as big as Texas. Sumatra was called the "sleeping giant" because it was so rich in cultures and resources, and so unknown.

West of Sumatra, are several chains of smaller islands. The largest of these is Nias, which is noted for having one of the most highly developed megalithic cultures in the world. Nias is larger than Rhode Island and almost as large as Delaware, but compared to its neighbor, Sumatra, it is a bird on the back of a buffalo. And Sumatra is only the third largest island in Indonesia.

How could such an immense area be so little known?

One reason may be that for over 300 years, Indonesia was the Dutch East Indies, and what was written about Indonesia was mostly in Dutch. If you're not Dutch, you probably don't read Dutch.

Another reason may be that the Dutch East Indian Company was not into nation building. It was into business. As long as the rubber and the spices and the teak and the oil kept moving out, the Dutch East Indian Company left the native social systems and customs alone, letting the peoples rule themselves in their traditional ways, and taking action only if something interfered with business.

They made no attempt to unite the islands. That would have been counterproductive. Instead, Indonesia became a vast anthropological museum, with almost every kind of society, from the fierce Dyacks of Borneo to the charming Balinese, from the stylized complexities of the Javanese aristocracy to the timid jungle Kubus who don't even have villages but move from place to place in small family groups.

The Dutch built roads and made some efforts in public health. They provided a series of hostels for Dutch businessmen and their families, some of which places survived the war and were the rest houses that Bob and I found useful. They made an attempt at universal schooling by providing public education through the third grade. Unfortunately, three years of schooling is not long enough to retain literacy.

The Japanese took Indonesia in 1942. After the war, the Dutch tried to reclaim their old empire. The result was revolution.

By 1950, when the Dutch conceded defeat, Indonesia's infrastructure was a shambles. The roads were impassable, the schools were closed, and the vast plantations of rubber and copra and tea and coffee were neglected and overgrown. Many of my students at the Methodist English School were old enough to be in college, but their educations had been interrupted by the war.

The new government faced enormous problems, and it didn't even have a formalized national language. Dutch was not an option for obvious reasons, and it wasn't politically wise to favor one of the principal existing languages like Javanese or Sundanese. But Malay, a language spoken in parts of South Sumatra and down the Malay Peninsula, was the trader's patois in ports throughout south East Asia. This formed the base for a new language, Bahasa Indonesia.

Before we left the States, the company gave us a two-week immersion course in Bahasa. This was necessary because almost no one in Indonesia knew any English. Most educated Indonesians were tri-lingual. They spoke their local dialect, Dutch and Bahasa.

Bahasa was a language in process. Every month, the government sent out a list of new words for everybody to learn.

Indonesian standards of education differed from ours, too. A fifth grade education brought respect. A high school education had the prestige of a master's degree. In all of Indonesia, there were fewer than 7,000 students in college.

Looking back, I realize that many of the Indonesians we encountered on our trip didn't know much more Bahasa than we did.

So why did we want to go to Nias? The oil camp was comfortable; neat cottages with mown lawns, a club, a swimming pool, a company school and a company store.

Why weren't we satisfied to travel the well-worn paths of Singapore, Bali, Jokgakarta and Bandung?

Why Nias?

I suppose I owe it to my archeologist grandfather and my minister father, and to all the missionaries who moved through my childhood, leaving dreams of distant places and other ways of thought. I owe it to Margaret Mead and Ruth Benedict, whose works Bob and I both read in high school, and to James Frazier's *The Golden Bough*. And there was Bob's brother-in-law, Conrad Bentzen, who made documentaries and showed us how to use a camera.

Why go to Nias? Because we wanted a conversation with a sleeping giant.

I have changed some names in this letter, edited a few rough spots and broken it into chapters for easier reading. Otherwise it is as it was written almost fifty years ago.

Today Sumatra is in the news, but it took a tsunami to do it. Seismic disturbances near and just off Nias have rocked the world. Thousands are dead, and thousands more are homeless. Scientists throughout the world are working, trying to understand the dynamics of our planet.

A Nias warrior could have told them. Latura, spirit of the underworld, is moving in his sleep.

Acknowledgements

Thanks to Sharlyn and John Heron, Jean and Earnest Howell, Barbara Murray and Mary Bentzen for their editorial suggestions and support, to Kirk Gould and Yvonne Murray for their knowledge of Adobe systems and to Rachel Murray for her skill with a keyboard, to Jon McWilliams for his guidance through the maze of electronic publishing, to the ladies of the LAUMC for getting me back to my keyboard, and to my wonderful husband and co-adventurer, Bob, who, when he wasn't holding my hand or reading manuscript, was creating all the maps.

1

The Plan

Palembang,
Sumatra,
Indonesia
September, 1956

Dear Folks,

We just got back from Nias.

You can find Nias on a large world map or a small map of Indonesia. It is the second farthest west of the islands off the coast of Sumatra.

We knew about Nias before we came to Sumatra. We heard about it from our anthropology friends and read about it in Loeb's *Sumatra*. Nias has one of the oldest isolated megalithic cultures known to exist. It may go back as far as 1500 B.C. It has been suggested that Nias was Marco Polo's "Island of Gold".

Like the Stonehenge people, the Niha erected ceremonial stones. They also took heads, but more of that later. The point is that, according to Loeb, the Niha were practicing their old religion as late as the 1930's! Loeb has a picture of a chief's house in Bawa Matalua, a wide, tall-roofed place with carved stones out front. That would be something to see! And what a wonderful name! "Bawa Matalua"! Say it slowly and it sings!

We'd been trying to get to Nias for almost a year, ever since a Dutch friend told us of going there when she was a child. She remembered dances and lots of stairs, but she didn't remember any gold. Maybe they'd run out.

We didn't care about gold. Was it still possible to go to the island?

Possible, but not easy. There were no deep-water ports, and the residents didn't welcome strangers. Our friend said that, except for missionaries and maybe a copra trader or two, we might be the first white people to get to Nias since the war. We could hardly wait!

This may be a long letter because it will be full of things that weren't what they were supposed to be.

It may be several letters because, as you know, our letters must be limited in size.

Here goes.

You may remember our references to Bangun Harahap, the huge Batak man who was an officer in the revolution. I told you he'd started a travel service after herding us to Ranau and Jokjakarta. Now he's started a construction company in order to make a living. We think we know why.

Bangun was delighted to arrange our tour to Nias. It would be complicated, he said, because Bawa Matalua was in the south of Nias, and most shipping goes to Gunung Sitoli in the center. But not to worry. There was less than eighty miles between the two.

Everything was set for the 25th of August.

We made sure that our gibbon, Hamlet, and our parakeet, George, would be properly cared for.

We checked the date on our identity cards, dug out our passports and packed our bags. We packed all the paraphernalia that one takes to unknown places in Indonesia: anti-dysentery medicine, aspirin, bandages, iodine, and anti-biotic salve. We took seasick pills and anti-malaria pills and on the advice of Bangun, a cache of canned food. I took batik skirts and shirts, pedal pushers and sandals, tennis shoes for hiking, and a couple of sarongs for sleeping. We put in Bob's little chess set because Indonesians like chess, and I added my dictionary, a notebook and pencils.

Harahap tours are supposed to include everything, but, just in case, we made a list of everything we might possibly have to pay for on the way, doubled the price, got the money and split it between us.

Then, aware that we might have to carry our own baggage, Bob the engineer embarked on a task. He made sure that everything was encased in something with a strap or a handle, and we tested the system.

"I feel like a coat-rack," I said.

"Can you manage?"

I could manage.

We practiced.

On the 24th of August, I was in the hospital with dysentery.

The doctor said that, as we were taking our local leave, he'd let me out the next day if I promised to eat "nasi tim" and take my pills like a good girl. Nasi tim is a revolting concoction of rice boiled down to a jelly that slides through your intestines like a sled on slush.

While I was promising to do anything to get to Nias, Bob was telling Bangun that I couldn't possibly go because I was ill. Could we postpone everything for a week?

"Sure!" said Bangun, "Easiest thing in the world."

I was furious.

For a week we lived with packed bags. Then at the last minute, Bangun couldn't go. The General was sick and needed him, he said, but there was nothing to worry about. He had a connection in Padang, a Mr. Huang, who would take care of everything.

Mr. Huang would book us on the Dutch KPM boat that went from Padang to Nias twice a week. When we got to Padang we were to tell Mr. Huang when we would be getting back so that he could book us on a plane from Padang back to Palembang. Mr. Huang would get us reservations at the Muara Hotel in Padang, and if after our sojourn in Nias we wanted to rest at a beauty spot called Bukit Tinggi, then Mr. Huang would arrange that, too. Mr. Huang would meet us at the airport in Padang, and the KPM boat would be waiting for us in the harbor.

Bob asked, "Who is this Mr. Huang?"

Bangun reached for a word in English. "He's a…what do you call it?…a hustler?"

Bangun's English sometimes verges on the inspired.

I forgot to tell you that, after we had dysentery at Ranau, lived through that rain in the jungle, had that mix-up with the Sultan of Jogjakarta, and experienced a tiger, I was, perhaps uncharitably, cautious about Harahap tours. I took advantage of the extra week to add a safety net.

The new head of the Information Office of South Sumatra was a graduate of the Methodist English School where I teach. His name is Mr. Tobing. I wanted his advice about Nias, and I hoped he might give us a letter permitting us to take pictures. It's always a good idea to carry a letter from a government agency. Even people who can't read recognize an official seal.

Mr. Tobing wasn't in, but his assistant was. The assistant assured us that Mr. Tobing would be happy to help, and there would be a letter waiting for us to pick up the next day.

I said I would send someone to get it.

He said that would be fine.

After I left the Information Office, I went to see Bangun. He was his usual jovial self until I asked if he would mind picking up Mr. Tobing's letter. He seemed hurt. He said that of course he would get us the letter if we wanted it, but Mr. Huang was going to provide an English speaking guide so what did we want with the Information Office? Later, he told Bob that he couldn't figure out what was wrong with me. I was usually so nice! They decided that it must have been the dysentery.

To tell the truth, Bob and I really wanted official permission to film Nias. Some of our pictures had been pretty good, so we wanted to turn producer for two weeks. Very serious!

We had our old Victor 16mm, and Bob had bought me a Bolex from a friend who was going home. We had the loan of a tape recorder, and even managed, with great difficulty, to import 12 rolls of 16mm color film. We had recording tape. We were going to go to Nias and stay long enough to learn about the people and accomplish something!

Did I tell you that Bob wants to get into the Explorers Club?

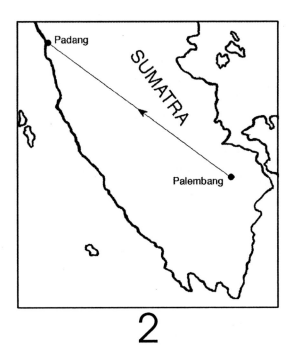

2

To Padang

Bangun was at the airport to see us off. It was all very jovial. The inverter and the tape recorder didn't weigh as much as we had expected. The two movie cameras and the still camera were passed through without being weighed at all. We sang as we marched to the plane.

The trip to Padang was lovely. Our plane was a two-engine Dakota. We flew over mountains and jungles and rivers and past Sumatra's tallest peak that sat bathed in clouds, contemplating its navel.

Across the aisle from us sat a man and his wife whom we took to be Dutch, but after a bit, the woman, a heavy, blousy, comfortable type of about fifty, leaned across and said in broad American, "I know where I saw you. You were Patty in 'Blue Moon'."

Yes, our camp's little theater had taken a play, "The Moon is Blue", to Djakarta. I said that indeed I had played Patty.

"I thought so! I'm Mary Keeler."

Mary Keeler and I talked all the rest of the way when we weren't admiring the scenery. Her husband was a dollar-a-year man with the I.C.A. educational program, which is part of the Marshall Plan. We've run into several of these people, and they are always interesting. It takes a certain kind of person to donate their valuable time and expertise for the token payment of a dollar a year!

One of Mr. Keeler's jobs was to locate promising students and send them for advanced study in the States. I told him I taught at the Methodist English School. We compared notes.

The Keelers said that they traveled on every available weekend and were heading to Bukit Tinggi where they had borrowed a house. We exchanged invitations to see each other, then the plane swung around a mountain and down into the basin of Padang in one of those breathtaking landings that Garuda Airlines loves so much.

Mr. Huang was a slight, nervous Chinese with a twitch. We sat down for coffee while waiting for our baggage. He put down his briefcase, twitched a smile, and said, "It is impossible for you to go to Nias.

"Impossible! Why?"

No boats.

No boats? What about that KPM ship that Bangun said went to Nias twice a week?

Bangun had misunderstood. There wasn't a boat twice a week. There used to be one every two weeks but it had stopped running. There wasn't any boat at all, but not to worry. We would go to Bukit Tinggi instead. Americans love Bukit Tinggi. We'd stay in Bukit Tinggi for two weeks. Then we would return to Palembang, and everyone would be happy. Mr. Huang had even booked us in at the rest house.

We said we didn't want to go to Bukit Tinggi. We wanted to go to Nias.

Mr. Huang said we'd be better off in Bukit Tinggi because the English-speaking guide he had promised us was not available for the stated price.

We repeated that we didn't want to go to Bukit Tinggi, we wanted to go Nias, and if we didn't have an English-speaking guide, we'd just have to try to use Indonesian.

Mr. Huang brightened. He said it was lucky we knew some Indonesian because if we ever did get to Nias, he knew a guide who could translate from

Niha to Indonesian and knew the island like a book. In the meantime, we'd be better off in Bukit Tinggi.

We said if he couldn't get us to Nias, would he take us to the Information Office?

Mr. Huang looked pained. There was, he said, no Information Office in Padang.

We said that was strange as we had a letter to it. Then we picked up our luggage, cameras, tape recorder, duffel bag, airline bag and all and staggered out to get a cab.

Mr. Huang was right behind us. He climbed in the front seat and tried to give instructions to the driver, but Bob broke in. "Information Office," he said.

The driver took us to the Information Office.

We had been informed in Palembang that the Information Office in Padang had English-speaking employees. This was only partially true. The director spoke a little bit of English, but he had trouble understanding it. We were in the same boat with Indonesian, so our conversation was conducted in both languages. He spoke ours, and we spoke his.

He said there was no regular boat from Padang to Nias because most boats sail out of Sibolga, up the coast. And the trip would be difficult because of the rainy season.

We have a genius for managing to travel in the rainy season. We thought we would miss it on this trip, but it seems that it comes a month earlier on the east coast. Still, a rainy season should be an inconvenience, not a deterrent. We said we wanted to go anyhow, so the Padang Information Officer gave us a letter to the Information Office in Sibolga and one to the Information Office on Nias. We thanked him for his help.

Mr. Huang lurked the in the background through all of this, trying to take charge and confused by the way things had gotten out of hand. He kept muttering that we should go to the hotel. He'd made reservations. We were expected. And he'd left his bicycle there. We thanked the Information Office man and let Mr. Huang direct our taxi to the Muara Hotel, where we registered. Mr. Huang went off on his bicycle.

The Muara Hotel was a sprawling colonial structure draped with bougainvilleas. It had a shady verandah, a dark lobby with ceiling fans, a sun-drenched dining room, a rice-based menu and a wonderful manager, an old Dutch woman who'd gone completely shapeless and wandered around in a Mother Hubbard and bedroom slippers.

We had just finished lunch when Mr. Huang reappeared. Behind him trotted a short skinny man with a completely blank expression. Mr. Huang introduced him as the Niha guide. We ordered tea.

One thing I will always remember about this trip is that every time we turned around we were drinking tea and passing out cigarettes. Bob and I were trying to stop smoking. We had an idea that the farther we got from Western influence, the easier it would be to escape nicotine. This is not true. The farther one gets into the wilderness, the higher the tobacco consumption until, when you get to where people carry spears and wear almost nothing, they start chain smoking at the age of six and make like chimneys until they expire. We've been places where there are no restaurants at all, no teashops, no clothing or grocery stores, but there was a smoke stall where you could buy three different brands.

Back to my story.

So we sat down with tea and cigarettes and listened to Mr. Huang extol the virtues of his companion. This man, he said, was born and bred on Nias, knew every inch of the place, and, if we ever managed to get to Nias, he would stay with us through thick and thin for the pittance of a hundred rupiahs a day plus food.

We tried to talk to this paragon. Turned out he was from North Nias and wanted to go home. When we said we wanted to go to Bawa Matalua, he thought we said we wanted to go to the Batu Islands. He remembered that Telak Dalam was a port in South Nias, but when he tried to draw a map, his geography was terrible. Then he said he'd work for eighty rupiahs a day and no food, and when would he start? We said that our plans were uncertain, but if we needed him we'd let Mr. Huang know.

He left.

Mr. Huang offered to take us shopping. He knew some very nice shops.

When we said we'd rather go to a market, Mr. Huang offered to hire us a pony cart so he could accompany us on his bicycle.

We said we would prefer to take a cab.

Mr. Huang offered to find us one. It would only cost 50 rupiahs an hour!

Bob got one in front of the hotel for 30 rupiahs.

We left Mr. Huang standing beside his bicycle, and went to the office of the Dutch shipping line, KPM, to find out what was really going on with boats.

The KPM agent was taking a nap, but he got up to give us tea and cigarettes. He confirmed what we already had heard. There was no boat stopping at Nias until the tenth, and then it went the wrong direction. Our only chance to get to Nias was to go to Sibolga and gamble on getting a coastal vessel from there. To get to Sibolga, we would have to take a bus. Buses aren't comfortable, and the road could be better. The journey would take two days. The agent gave us the kind of handshake you get from funeral directors and advised us, if we tried the trip, to take pillows.

Bob left me at the hotel and went to the bus station to investigate first hand. He came back shaking his head. We could get a bus to Bukit Tinggi and another from there to Sibolga, but it would be hard on the equipment. Besides, everyone said the journey took a day and a half, except for one hot-rod with fire in his eye who said that, for a sizable bonus, he'd dash through in a day. Bob declined his offer.

We sat down in the lounge to talk things over.

Mother Hubbard shuffled by and overheard us. She volunteered that the Harbormaster of Padang was staying in the hotel, and he might know about transport to Nias. She pointed out his room.

He wasn't the Harbormaster. He was an inspector from Djakarta, but he was helpful. In his official capacity, he said that there were no registered ships going from Padang to Nias. But, he added off the record, there might be unregistered ones. They sneaked up at another anchorage. There were little motorboats, too, but he wouldn't recommend them because they tended to sink.

He had heard that there was a new Catholic school in South Nias, and they might have a boat. He suggested that we talk to the Catholic mission next door. We thanked him and went to the mission.

A white-clad nun ushered us in. We said, "Good evening, sister."

She spoke no English. She was Dutch. So, in Indonesian, we told her we wanted to go to Nias. She glowed. "So do I!" She wilted. "But I wasn't chosen." She asked us if, when we got to South Nias, would we give her greetings to the sisters there? We said we would do better. We would carry a letter.

The sister directed us to the rectory across the street. Several Indonesian men were playing chess on the porch. We asked where the pastor was. One of the men went to the door and called. We heard a bass trill of an answer, and a moment later, a bath-robed man with moustache and goatee came swinging down the hall. He wrung our hands. We said, "Good evening, father."

He said, in Italian, that he spoke Italian, in French that he spoke French, in German that he spoke German, in Spanish that he spoke Spanish, and in Indonesian that he did not speak English. So we tried Indonesian.

The priest was fascinated by the fact that we wanted to go to Bawa Matalua, but he wasn't encouraging. Yes, his mission had a boat, but it was broken. He seemed to think that if we got to Nias, we were unlikely to be able to get back.

We said that there was a KPM ship back from Nias that really was on a regular schedule.

He shook his head and forefinger like a metronome set at largo and looked very sad. "In Indonesia," he said, "they have forgotten their watches."

Next he boomed over to one of the chess players whom he introduced as an expert on shipping. He explained to the shipper that in France they had time, in Italy they had time, in China they had time, in Africa they had time, but in Indonesia, they had no time. All clocks were forgotten. Why was that, he wanted to know.

Before the man could answer, the father turned back and said that a month ago his fellow priest had gone to visit their mission on the island of Enggano.

"He said he'd be right back." The father gave a huge shrug with hands upheld at his chest. "Not yet." Then "Excuse," he said and dashed off to reappear a moment later wearing a white cassock that billowed out behind him. "So?" he raised his eyebrows into a black, questioning arc.

We said we thought we might go by way of Sibolga.

That was possible, he said, but it was a long, hard trip. There was an awfully nice father there who…"If you get there, give him my greetings…but I digress…If you go to Sibolga and come back by way of Sibolga, then you may spend your whole time going back and forth to Sibolga, so…" He sat back, hands folded, a pixie smile on his face. Then he turned to me and looked soulful. Head on one side he breathed, "Sometimes I wish I weren't a priest." He winked.

The nun came by with her letter to her friends on Nias, and Bob said that we'd better be getting back to the hotel. The father gripped our hands and wished us luck. As we were halfway down the steps Bob dug back into our Greenwich Village days and dredged up, "Arrivederci."

The priest sparkled. "Arrivederci, pal!" he roared. We left him silhouetted against the light of the porch, his hand up in blessing.

Next morning Mr. Huang was back. What would we be doing today?

We told him that we had appreciated his help but we would be going to Sibolga, so we didn't need him any more.

He brightened. Bukit Tinggi was on the way to Sibolga. He had already made bookings for us at the rest house. He could go with us and show us the sights. However, it would be difficult to get a cab for less than six hundred rupiahs.

We decided to try the bus station.

Good! He knew a place at the bus station that rented cars.

Off we went in a pony cart with Mr. Huang pedaling along behind us.

The bus station was a wide place in the street, with stalls and shops thick along the sides and buses parked all up and down, each with its own universe of gesticulating passengers, squalling peddlers, and small, ragged and very curious street boys.

Indonesian buses are in no way related to the luxurious conveyances that waft around the states. Here, buses are trucks with cabins built on their chassis and plank seats arranged to get as many people as possible into the smallest space.

While Mr. Huang was arguing with a bus driver, Bob found a car that would take us to Bukit Tinggi for two hundred rupiahs. It was new and luxurious, and the driver said we could stop and look at things along the way. We went back to the hotel to get our things. Mr. Huang made arrangements for the hotel to keep his bicycle, and we started off.

To get to Bukit Tinggi, you cut into the mountains and follow a deep gorge called "Buffalo Canyon". We passed Minangkabau houses with curved roofs and bright gardens. Most were palm-thatched but every once in a while we saw one with a rusty corrugated iron roof.

"I wish they didn't do that," I said.

"Iron very good," said Mr. Huang. "Lasts longer and keeps out insects and snakes and small animals."

"But thatch is so pretty."

"Iron better," said Mr. Huang.

The air grew cooler and fresher as we got higher. We saw a lovely waterfall. Then we rounded a corner and entered another atmosphere. The air stank like something was rotting. "It's a rafflesia flower," said Mr. Huang, proudly.

The rafflesia is the biggest flower in the world and only lasts for a few days, so it's a privilege to find one in bloom. We stopped the car and braved the smell to look. The bloom lay down from the side of the road in a cluster of vegetation. It was over a yard wide and shaped like a huge reddish apple blossom with five bulbous petals around a circular center. It looked more like a fungus than a flower, and smelled like something that has been dead for a while. It is named after Thomas Raffles who founded Benkulen and modern Singapore. I wonder if that was a compliment.

The rest of the trip was beautiful. We stopped for lunch at a lovely alpine style resort that belonged to a cousin of Mr. Huang. He offered to get us a good price on a cottage. We said no.

When we pulled up to the rest house in Bukit Tinggi, Mr. Huang offered to stay and show us around. We declined, but thanked him for his help. There were a few nervous minutes before he made one ominous last effort. "If you come back after all…" he began.

We smiled him on his way. We'd been on Harihap tours before. Sometimes you're better off on your own.

Bukit Tinggi

Buffalo Canyon

Minangkabau Roofs

Market

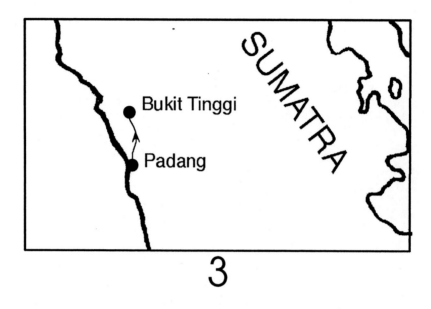

3

Bukit Tinggi

Bukit Tinggi is the largest town in the Minangkabau highlands. The Minangkabau are one of the few surviving matriarchal cultures. Family names and family wealth are passed down through the female line. Minangkabau women walk proudly.

The Minangkabau have their own distinct art forms, colorful and intricate decorations woven into their fabrics and carved into the walls and columns of their houses. Their roofs curve up into horns like the curve of the horns of a water buffalo. "Minangkabau" means "the people of the buffalo".

Bukit Tinggi sits on a hill. "Bukit Tinggi" means "high hill". At the very top, there is a lovely old Minangkabau house that has been converted into a museum.

Pedicabs and pony carts lazed along the streets looking for passengers. The first thing we did after checking into the rest house was to hire a pony cart to take us to the museum.

As we went up the street, we heard a big "Hello!" We looked up. There was Mrs. Keeler, the woman from the airplane, waving out a window. She offered to show us the town.

We hired another pony cart. Mr. and Mrs. Keeler are large people, and we felt a twinge of sympathy as the cart squawked and settled back on its two wheels, and the little pony put down his head and strained to get up the hill.

We saw the museum. It was beautiful. We walked around the park and admired the view. Then I went with the Keelers back to their house, while Bob went off to see if he could find transportation to Sibolga.

We talked about the Marshall Plan and the I.C.A. and how they were doing. Mr. Keeler asked if we would like to meet some of their students. He and Mrs. Keeler were invited to an orchestra rehearsal where some former I.C.A. students were playing. Would we like to go?

"A gamelan orchestra?"

"No. They're exploring western music."

I accepted for both of us.

About an hour later, Bob came back. He was wearing a broad smile.

"Come outside," he said, "I want you to meet someone."

Parked in front of the Keeler's house was a battered, battle-scarred bus. In front of it stood three men and a boy. "These gentlemen would like to take us to Sibolga," Bob said. "They're giving us a trial ride home."

I looked at the gentlemen.

The biggest was a huge Batak with a three-day beard. His shirt was torn and his teeth gleamed like a cannibal's.

Beside him stood an evil-looking character with a shock of uncut hair and a red kerchief around his head.

The third man had a high-cheekboned face that would have looked at home in a ghost story. He wore a blood-red shirt, and his eyes were cat-like slits against the sun.

The fourth character was a boy of about ten. He had a wide little face, a big straw hat and a smile that would melt the heart of the devil. He looked like Tom Sawyer.

"Peace," I said, and got in the bus.

This is how Bob described his afternoon.

The Bukit Tinggi bus depot was a large area in front of the market. There were buses from everywhere, and "barkers" who grabbed people's shoulders and shouted the virtues of their vehicles. Bob learned that most buses won't make the

Sibolga run in the rainy season. He asked about a private car, but decided that would cost too much.

He saw a smaller depot partway down the hill. No luck there, either, but one man suggested Bob try a dispatching office down the way. He had his boy lead Bob through all sorts of byways to a dingy parking lot.

There was The Martimbang Bus Company! It had a paragon of a bus leaving for Sibolga at noon the very next day. Greatest bus! Greatest driver! And because we carried sensitive equipment, they would (albeit illegally, as one is supposed to put all heavy baggage on top) sell us the entire plank bench behind the driver. This was the equivalent of five whole seats! And the trip wouldn't take two full days. It would take only ten hours to reach Padang Sidempuan, where there was a rest house where we would stay until morning. After that, it was only two hours more to Sibolga.

They would pick us up in the morning so we wouldn't have to go down to the depot, and, to prove the travel-worthiness of their vehicle, they would drive us back to the rest house.

"How could I refuse?" asked Bob.

"How indeed!"

After dinner, the Keelers picked us up to go the rehearsal. We heard the orchestra before we entered the house. They were playing Mozart. They didn't stop as we slipped into our chairs.

They worked hard, pausing to correct faulty passages or problems with intonation. Only the lead violinist and the pianist were advanced players. The rest were about high school level. Occasionally their love of the music outreached their ability, but on the whole it was nice.

The musicians took a break, and out came lemonade and conversation. Everyone spoke English, and I particularly liked the wife of the conductor. She was an Indonesian woman who didn't fade into the woodwork around Americans. Her name was Sadiah.

Conversation was quick and varied. Here is an example.

"Sadiah should run for Parliament."

"Me? Why?"

"You're pretty, you're a Minangkabau woman, and you talk a lot."

"What do you expect me to say?"

"What we tell you to." Laughter.

Sadiah's husband: "You try. She doesn't listen to me."

"That won't matter. Nobody will listen to her anyway. She's polluted."

"I'm polluted? How am I polluted?"

"You've studied in America. You're polluted."

I asked where they had learned to play, and found that only the conductor had formal training. Before the war, he'd studied violin with a Dutch teacher. He taught the others, and now they all teach each other.

"You know our saying, 'Tolong menolong?'"

"Yes. It means, 'Give help, receive help.'"

"That's right. We 'tolong menolong' with music."

They returned to their rehearsal. I took a deep breath of frangipani-scented air and sat back to enjoy. Who would have thought I would end this day listening to Mozart on a mountain?

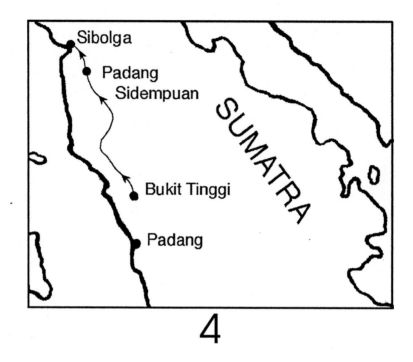

4

The Martimbang Bus Company

Next morning we went to the market to buy supplies. We wanted some light mattresses on which to rest our equipment, and I wanted eating utensils. Besides, we like markets.

The Bukit Tinggi market overlooks a lovely valley. There are steps going down through a huge Minangkabau gate on which a little boy was whittling when we passed. The market was fragrant with the smells of spices and sandalwood, durian and garlic, incense and hibiscus and fresh baked bread. We walked between rows of canvas-roofed stalls. Merchants peered out over piles of fruit or splashes of batiks spread out like wash on a line.

Men gathered on the street to smoke and laugh and chew betel. Women in bright kains passed with market baskets and little knitted shopping bags. Barefoot children chased each other around people's legs. The ground was soft with dust and must have felt wonderful and warm to bare feet. A shy little girl, all eyes and almost losing her kain around her tiny hips, peered at us over a pile of gaudy men's shorts. A naked baby rolled around on the floor, while his mother squatted beside him, smiling with betel-blackened teeth.

Metallic hammering rang from the makers of pots and pans, and the voices of chickens and goats and ducks joined in from the meat stalls. The place rang with bargaining, gossip, and argument.

We had difficulty with the Minangkabau dialect. This attracted a crowd of people who could speak both Minangkabau and Indonesian and wanted to help.

A man in a kitchenware stall asked five rupiahs apiece for a knife, two spoons, two cups and a little pail for carrying food or cooking. We left, five minutes later, with all we needed for six rupiahs.

We had a terrible time finding mattresses. We passed line after line of men whirring manual sewing machines before we found them right behind where we had started.

We bought two children's mattresses and a "Dutch wife", a bolster-like affair that looked as though it would make good support for our equipment. We also bought rope, a basket to carry things and some fruit to munch on our way home. We wound our way down the hill to the hotel and lunch.

At noon, the Martimbang bus ground up the hill to our door. We climbed in and said goodbye to the English language.

I smiled nervously at everybody, tied our cameras and the tape recorder to the seat, and we drove back to the bus station to pick up the rest of the passengers. They were all men.

Tom Sawyer climbed on top of the bus, and the red-kerchiefed character tossed luggage up for him to tie on. We lurched off.

Bob got out his chess set and began a game with one of the passengers. Most Indonesians adore chess. Even if you can't speak to each other, chess breaks the ice.

We drove along the bottom of Buffalo Canyon. The road was about the size of a driveway because a stream took up most of the room, so when we faced a vehicle going in the opposite direction, there was much backing up and maneuvering. We went through little hamlets of Minangkabau houses. We passed a rice-flour mill with a big, wooden waterwheel. A worker in a straw hat leaned against the wall watching the grindstone go around.

We left the stream and twisted up through mountain jungle. It began to rain, and I learned why buses didn't like this road in the wet. There was no wall beside the road. Our windshield wipers clank-clanked in vain because the deluge obscured any view. We slithered and lurched and tipped, and I couldn't see whether there was enough brush to stop our fall if we slipped and tumbled down the mountainside.

At last the sun broke through, and we emerged in the highlands at the edge of Batak country.

About a hundred years ago, Bataks ate people. They didn't eat just anybody. They only ate enemies and criminals. And they didn't just kill them and cook them. They tied them to a pole and danced around them and got all worked up about how evil they were. There was only one way to get rid of such evil without freeing it to do more evil. Devour it! At a frenzied point in the dance, someone would take a bite. Others joined, and, bite by bite, the victim was eaten alive.

During the last century, a couple of Lutheran missionaries went to Batak territory. The Batak priests declared them evil because they spoke against the old gods and dared look upon the sacred lake. So they ate them. Later, the Bataks worried about whether they should have eaten people who hadn't done them any harm. So when more missionaries came along, the Bataks embraced Christianity, and the cannibalized missionaries became martyrs, personal Christs whose lives had been given for the Bataks.

I reminded myself that that was a long time ago.

Every once in a while we stopped to pick up or discharge passengers. It worked this way. An advance man stood beside the road waving like mad. The bus screamed past, stopping as fast as it could. The man ran up and asked where we were going. If the answer was satisfactory, he climbed aboard and rode to where the passengers were waiting.

Our number was constantly changing. Every time we stopped, Tom Sawyer scrambled up to tie on the baggage. He sat beside the back door, and sometimes we'd roar off with Tom clinging to his seat and his legs swinging back in the breeze until he could pull himself through.

Once a whole wedding party got on board. They stood shoved together like subway riders at rush hour, with baskets of food held over their heads, swaying in unison with the lurching of the bus. They didn't ride more than a mile before they called out "stop" and all piled out into the crowd waiting to welcome them.

"Ado," called Tom Sawyer, and off we went.

The sun was low in the sky when we stopped for supper at an open restaurant. I waited in the bus, while Bob bought some rice cakes and tea. We shared our cookies with the other passengers.

I needed a ladies' room. This posed a problem because I didn't wear a kain. Sarongs and kains have a double purpose. It is possible to be modest in the open. But I was wearing pedal pushers, and there were no women to ask what to do.

Bob realized my problem and, after much talk with various rough-looking characters during which he collected a delighted crowd, he managed to locate a "little room" at the back of the restaurant. Everyone helped chase out its occupants, then I was summoned and ushered regally through a crowd that made way with nods and smiles and gestures of direction. Scarlet-faced, I smiled my thanks and entered. The little room was open to the sky, with no plumbing except an oilcan of water and an open drainage ditch that disappeared under the fence. No door. I checked the sight lines to the restaurant.

As I started back, I heard a small cheer. Peering over the top of the fence was a group of waving children. I hadn't noticed that the road, which was higher than the restaurant, ran just on the other side of the fence. I waved back. I was getting pretty blasé.

We climbed back on the bus and drove on.

Darkness fell. Black jungle flickered green in our headlights then swished by my open window, so close that I could have picked a leaf. We were probably the only white people within miles. I remembered those missionaries. I began to get a headache.

We were stopped at a police point. The police wanted to know our business and look at our papers. We showed them, and they let us pass. We went on a bit and were stopped again. Were they checking on foreigners? How patient was our Batak driver? My headache grew worse.

We pulled out of the second police check and into the black jungle-fringed night. Someone began to sing. Others joined in, and soon the whole bus was bursting with rhythm. The song was the "Battle Hymn of the Republic", sung in Batak.

There was our Tom Sawyer, his eyes sparkling, his straw hat swinging back and forth to the music, his grin wider than ever. Next to him, bandana-top, eyes lifted to the ceiling, boomed out harmony. The driver sang bass.

The next song was "Oh Come All Ye Faithful". We joined in. Then came "Silent Night".

The driver leaned back. "Kami Kristen juga!" he said, "We are Christian, too."

We sang for hours. They sang in Indonesian. We sang in English. They sang us hymns we didn't know, and we sang them hymns they didn't know. We were still singing as we pulled into the rest house at Padang Sidempuan. We had traveled together. We were friends.

Bob and I were the only passengers to stay at the rest house. The others disappeared to various havens.

The manager told us that two Americans had passed through only a week before. We were surprised. What Americans would be crazy enough to make such a difficult journey at such a bad time of year?

The answer was in the registration book. They were with United Nations Relief and were on their way to Sibolga.

A hillside had fallen on the town.

Next morning, the bus arrived at six sharp, with Tom Sawyer and his straw hat perched triumphantly on the roof waving at us. We threw up our bags. He caught them, secured them, and swung in through the back window as we pulled off into the dim pre-dawn to collect the rest of the passengers from their own overnight lodgings.

The morning mists cleared as we began our descent to the sea. We smelled wood fires and passed villagers on their way to their rice fields. We left Batak country and entered Tapanuli Province. We began to pass piles of broken rocks. We traveled a road yellow from newly cleared earth.

In two hours we were in Sibolga.

The Road to Sibolga

The Martimbang Bus Company

Street Scene

Supper

"Tom Sawyer"

Rest Stop

5

Sibolga and the Sea

The landslide had swept through the rural kampongs near the hills, but most of Sibolga lies on a ledge between the mountains and the sea, so the slide had missed the main part of town. Its only direct effect on us was that there were no rooms. The hotel was filled with disaster relief people. So was the rest house.

The Martimbang Bus Company tried to help us find lodging, but to no avail. They were behind schedule and had to go on. We waved goodbye and went into the bus station to call our good angels, the Information Office.

In no time at all, a nice young man came to get us. He said he was assistant to the Information Officer who was too busy to leave his office. We apologized for our inopportune arrival and expressed our sympathy for the disaster. He waved away our concern. "It makes work. The government pays."

He helped us lug our gear to the Information Office. It was a steaming day. All transportation was in use by the relief effort. An occasional car rushed past filled with uniformed men. We heard the roar of a bulldozer.

When we finally arrived, the officer greeted us with a nod and a handshake. He gave us tea and cigarettes and read our letter.

"This says to give you help. What do you need?"

We wanted to go to Nias, but more urgently, we needed a place to stay.

He had no jurisdiction on Nias. Transportation was the province of the Transportation Office and the Harbormaster. Housing was tight because of the emergency. He offered us a book on Nias, the only one he had. Obviously he didn't know what to do with us. He assigned his assistant to help us, and went back to work.

The assistant's name was Monsur. Monsur found us a place in the office to leave our things, and took us to make our duty calls, while the clerk in the Information Office tried to find us a room.

Before I go into this little dance of social calls, it might be a good idea to stop for a bit of explanation.

There are two words in Bahasa that don't translate well into English. One is "patut" which means proper, polite, customary and gracious.

The other word is "adat". Adat is the body of laws, customs and beliefs that defines the culture. Patut is courtesy, adat is tradition.

These concepts are important to know because if you stumble over something that's patut, you can be forgiven for your ignorance, but if you trespass on adat, the smiles may look the same, but all around you invisible doors silently close.

It is patut to make calls when you visit a new place.

You should check in with the police because they like to know who's in town. And you should call on the highest government officer in the district.

Often there is a traditional ruler, too, who may or may not be part of the formal government, but who is a very powerful man. His title may vary. He may be a chief or a sultan or a king, but whatever name he carries, he is the guardian of the adat.

In Sibolga we called on the Governor first. He had a very large office and a very large desk. He was wearing a black Indonesian fez and leaning back in a swivel chair smoking a black cigar. At the sides of the room, several staff members sat on the edge of their seats with their hands folded in their laps like students in the principal's office. When the Governor waved his cigar, they all leaped to attention. Then he'd smile at us proudly, like a general displaying his troops.

The Governor dispatched a staff member to ask about transportation to Nias. He personally checked with the hotel and appeared irritated when they told him they had no room. The staff member returned with the news that the government mail boat was in port. The Governor suggested that we see the Harbormaster. His cigar waved languidly, and we wafted out with the smoke.

Next stop was the police station. The Police Chief was a big, jolly fellow who joked all the time we were there. He said he was new in Tapanuli Province, but he seemed to enjoy it.

Time for breakfast. Monsur asked whether we wanted Chinese or Indonesian food, and seemed happy when we said Indonesian. Actually, we didn't care. We were staggering from fatigue, and I was developing another headache.

Monsur took us to an open-front food shop where we saw some of the staff members who had seen sitting on chairs at the Governor's office. They were much more relaxed and talkative, and said some things that I don't think the Governor would have liked to hear. The food was good: rice, sauces, curried eggs, fried onions, and a kind of soup that we'd never had before, all nice and hot.

Indonesian food tastes like pure fire the first time you have it, then, bit by bit, you get used to it, so that after a while other food seems tasteless by comparison.

After lunch, we walked down to the harbor. Sampans and outrigger canoes were anchored off shore with people fishing. Beyond them, several small islands stood between Sibolga and open sea.

Pulled up at the breakwater were several Chinese "coasters". These are little fifty-ton craft with over-slung rear ends and laundry hanging from the windows. Their superstructures are built on large, round hulls that would be hard to handle in heavy seas. We were willing to take one of them to Nias, dirty as they were, but Monsur said that he wouldn't ride one if his life depended on it. If a wave catches them wrong, they roll to the side and keep on rolling. Or termites get them. Or they catch fire from the open fires they use for cooking.

A long deep-water dock stretched into the harbor. Pulled up to it, was one of the prettiest little cruisers I've ever seen. It was perhaps 200 tons, gleaming white and slim as a destroyer. Mansur said it was the government boat that went to Nias with the mail.

Could we get on board? Would our letter from the Information Office be enough to do that? We went to the Harbormaster's office to ask.

The Harbormaster wasn't there. His assistant said that the mail boat had broken down and was in for repairs. He didn't know of any boats going to Nias, but maybe the Harbormaster did.

Monsur suggested that first we see if any shipping agents had chartered boats to go to Nias. By this time Bob's face was drawn, and my headache throbbed so much that when I stepped into the sun, everything swam.

We made the rounds of the agents. There was one ship going to Nias. The "Celia", a copra boat from Penang, was due in the next day. She was even going to Telak Dalam, the port closest to Bawa Matalua, but she wasn't going directly. First she would go Gunung Sitoli in central Nias. Then she would go to the Batu Islands for a load of copra. After that, she was going to Telak Dalam in South Nias.

We looked at the map in the Nias book. Why spend all that time on a boat? Once we got to Gunung Sitoli, it couldn't be over eighty miles to Telak Dalam. Surely we could manage that! We'd gotten from Bukit Tinggi to Sibolga, hadn't we? We'd just take the Celia for the first leg, from Sibolga to Gunung Sitoli.

The agent agreed, but there was a problem. The Celia didn't take passengers.

We staggered back to the Information Office.

They had found us a room. It was true that all the good hotel rooms and government billets were taken, but there was one place left. It wasn't luxurious. It was the second best Chinese hotel, but it was an approved billet for the Indonesian army.

Bob and I chorused, "We'll take it!"

Monsur helped us carry our things to a teashop and motioned us inside. There was litter on the floor and a wooden table down the side displaying cakes, cookies, and such. We passed a group of men reading newspapers and playing chess and gossiping or just sitting, and continued to the back where a large Chinese woman guarded an antiquated cash register. She took our money and turned us over to a small, bandy-legged Chinese man in shorts and "selops", the little wooden-soled slippers that go "ke-plop, ke-plop".

We thanked Mansur and followed our guide down a short hall, through a musty storeroom, and up a flight of stairs to a large room full of ragged rattan chairs, gossiping women and active children. In the back of this room was a narrow hall with doors on both sides and a light bulb hanging in the middle. The light bulb wasn't on because it wasn't dark yet. Regardless of how dim it was, electricity didn't go on until six-thirty.

The man stopped at the third door, opened it, stood aside, and we entered. He handed us a huge key that would have hung with dignity on the key ring of a medieval castle, and off he ke-ploped.

We sat down on the beds with a thud and looked around. The room was about eight by eight feet and held two beds, a dresser, and a table, all raw wood. Each bed was a wooden plank on legs, with boards around the edges to form a box for the kapok mattress. To one side was a tiny barred window, about twenty inches square, that looked out on the backs of some other buildings. The walls rose to within about a yard of the ceiling, then became screens.

We collapsed. Bob woke up at five in the afternoon. I woke up at six the next morning. We both felt fine.

The women we had seen on our way to our room were soldiers' wives. The bravest of them accosted me the next morning as I searched for a bathroom.

"Where from?"

"Palembang."

"Where to?"

"Nias."

"Why?"

Another women slipped up to listen. There was a torrent of rapid conversation. If it was Indonesian, it was too fast for me to understand.

The first woman turned back to me. "Why?" she repeated.

I tried to excavate enough Indonesian to explain, but could only produce, "We want to see it."

Another spate of incomprehensible speech.

The first woman asked if I wished to bathe.

I said I did.

She led me to an open balcony that was obviously used as a laundry. She showed me two little closed rooms, one for washing people, the other, the john. Across the room was a long table for cooking, for washing dishes, and just putting things.

If I needed to wash clothes, she said, I could use her bucket.

I thanked her and accepted.

And if I needed to cook, there was a burner.

I said we would probably eat downstairs.

We were to get to know these people. The screens above the walls provided both ventilation and recreation. We could hear everything, and we tested our Indonesian by eavesdropping.

The woman next door wanted to know how they would ever save any money if her husband didn't stop throwing it away.

The kid down the hall didn't want his supper. He didn't want to go to sleep, either. We got to know this child very well. He didn't want to do anything except devour candy, and his success was obvious by his Buddha-like proportions.

When I washed my clothes, the women clustered around watching and wanting to help. They asked me about America, and I corrected some propaganda-inspired notions. They compared their new democracy with ours and got into heated discussions amongst themselves.

They shared their tea with me.

They cleaned their quarters with a community broom and offered to sweep our room along with their own. I borrowed the broom, and they watched. They were amazed at how much stuff we had.

I had no problem gaining access to the john because one woman made this her particular province. Every time I appeared, she asked if I wanted to "throw away water". When I said "yes" she dashed off to chase out the children who were playing in the john. When I was safely inside, I could hear her cheerful voice caroling down the hall, telling everyone what I was doing.

At night Bob went down to the teashop to play chess and talk. This was a stag affair, and we women stayed away, except once when I played chess with Bob and attracted a crowd. One night I opened a can of chili and tried the cooking facilities. My little pail worked just fine.

We liked that hotel, which was lucky. We were there for three nights.

Our Indonesian got better and better, and we learned new words.

For example, in Indonesian, "betul" means "for sure." There is another word, "benar" that means "more for sure". Now we learned a third word, "pasti", that means "absolutely for sure". It can be "betul" that a ship will leave on the fifth. It can be "benar betul" that she will go to Gunung Sitoli. But if you ask, "Pasti?" you get a shrug. Who can guarantee fate?

On our second day at the hotel, the Harbormaster was in his office.

He was a lovely man, slender and dapper in a spotlessly white uniform with black and gold epaulettes that glittered in the sun. He had a little French moustache. When he went outside, he donned a white yachting cap, tilted at a rakish angle. He swaggered.

At first the Harbormaster claimed to know no English, so we spoke exclusively in Indonesian, except when Bob wanted to say something to me in a hurry, or vice versa. The last day we were in Sibolga, we discovered that the Harbormaster spoke excellent English. He just liked to eavesdrop.

He told us that the government boat would be repaired in three days, and if we wanted to wait until then, we could go over on her. That wouldn't give us much time in Bawa Matalua. And no one had any idea how we could get there from Gunung Sitoli, although everyone seemed confident that somehow we could. How much of this confidence was in shipping and how much in our determination, I don't know.

It was beginning to dawn on us that if ships were so rare, we might have trouble getting back from Nias to Padang and home. We thanked the Harbormaster for his help and went to the KPM office to confirm our return trip.

Yes, they had a KPM ship with passenger accommodations stopping at Nias. When we said we would be in South Nias, they said their ship would be stopping in Telak Dalam for copra just when we needed it. We could sail directly from there to Padang in time to make our flight back to Palembang the day that Bob's leave was up. Perfect!

We went to the Catholic mission to deliver our letter to the priest.

This priest was a middle-aged Dutch man named Father Johan. He was thin and had a little gray beard. He gave us a cup of tea, and we talked about Nias. Seemed that his mission had opened a new school in Telak Dalam, and he'd been boning up on the subject.

Where did the Niha come from? Father Johan showed us pictures of the Niha and of the people of Assam in the Himalayan foothills. The faces were almost identical, wider than most Malays and finely chiseled with high cheekbones, and their artifacts are almost identical with Niha artifacts. This gave credit to those who claim that the Niha migrated from Asia. But the Niha language is Malayo-Polynesian. How could that be? And if the Niha came from Assam, how much of their culture came from India, how much was developed on Nias and how had they managed to maintain it for so long?

He talked about the old Niha religion.

He said that animism is a powerful adversary.

The old people believed that everything from the smallest insect to the entire sky had an aware spirit. They were surrounded by myriads of spirits. Life was a constant negotiation with spirits. Some spirits, like the spirits of the dead, could be captured and kept in images or imprisoned in heads. Others ran free and had to be dealt with.

There were things one could do.

You could bribe spirits with sacrifices and rituals, dances and monuments.

You could protect yourself with charms and fetishes.

You could intimidate spirits with demonstrations of power, collections of heads, ostentatious displays, feasts and wars.

"But that's all past," I said, "isn't it?"

"We hope so, but animism is a strong evil. It wouldn't surprise me to find fresh heads in the back country."

Father Johan pointed out how the topography of the island makes it difficult to travel. "They don't welcome strangers. Without copra, there would be no reason for anyone to go there."

He told us that his sister was a nun at the new school there, but she was ill and there was no doctor. The only doctor on Nias was in Gunung Sitoli, and he couldn't get south because his boat was broken, too.

We suggested that one of the freighters might be able to bring his sister out.

That was not possible, he said, because she had broken her hip and was in traction. There were no deep-water docks on Nias. All the ships had to anchor off shore and load and unload with lighters.

Imagine lying with a broken hip in a tiny village in South Nias, with no doctor and no way of being moved!

Would we look her up if we got there, he asked.

Of course.

He wrote a letter for his sister and one for the priest in Telak Dalam. He said if we could get there, we could stay at the mission. There was no hotel.

"So now, we must get you there," he said.

Father Johan took us all over town. I don't know how he found the time, as he was running a school and was short-handed, but he strode along, an eager smile on his face, while we panted to keep up.

Sibolga is a harbor town, and much of it is warehouses and offices. He wandered in and out of them as if he were in his own rectory. He re-checked sources that we had already checked, and ferreted out others. No luck. He sat us down for another cup of tea.

He said our last hope was to try to book passage on the Celia even though she didn't take passengers. We told him that we could sleep on the deck. In that case, he said, we might have a chance. But don't count on it. The captain was French.

The next day the Celia came in. She was a pip-squeak of a freighter, but a freighter, nevertheless. She had a deck and wheelhouse aft, two little holds amidships and a little raised deck on the prow. That was all.

Monsur took us to the agent who had chartered the Celia. We sat down for tea and a sad story. The Celia had two passenger cabins, but the captain wouldn't release them. And the captain was French, so the agent didn't dare press the point. Maybe we should ride out and ask him ourselves.

We went down to the dock.

The man in charge of launches looked dubious. He said the Celia didn't take passengers and the captain never came ashore. He was French. Our boatman also warned us that the captain was French.

We rode out to the Celia and climbed up the rope ladder to her dock. The short dark man by the wheelhouse did a double take when he saw us. He said something to an Asian sailor who dashed off.

"Hello," we said.

"Alo," said the Captain. "I not use English good."

Okay, we'll speak Indonesian.

He didn't speak Indonesian either.

I couldn't remember a word of high school French. I tried, but it came out in Indonesian.

A moment later the sailor reappeared with a blond girl. She was the Captain's wife. Her name was Colette and she spoke a little English. The Captain's name was Gaston. How French can you get?

We were ushered to a table and chairs protected by a canopy, where we sat down to orange soda and broken conversation.

We explained our predicament.

The Captain shrugged and said that his passenger cabins were full of his own things.

We said we could sleep on the deck.

He seemed strangely reluctant for a man operating a ship in the tropics, where deck passage is common. He muttered something about white people and propriety, but at last he consented.

Happy, we went back to shore. What a fine life they had! Two young people running a freighter around in the tropics. What fun! We went in search of a French dictionary.

There were two bookstores in Sibolga. One only had Indonesian books. The other didn't have a French dictionary. I couldn't think of the word for grammar book, so I asked for a French schoolbook.

"Wah!" said the clerk, and dashed to the back of the store where he picked up several volumes, dashed back, and spread them proudly on the counter. "Nana," "Madame Bovary," "Devil in the Flesh." We said that wasn't what we had in mind.

There was shouting in the street. We went out to investigate. It was a labor disagreement about who was going to load...guess what ship? The Celia!

There was nothing we could do about that, so we went to buy a blanket, deck passage being what it is. We were at the market when Mansur came to tell us that the Bupati of Nias was staying at the big hotel. We should go to see him.

What was a bupati?

A bupati is like a governor. A bupati is the boss. A bupati is the keeper of the adat. This Bupati ran Nias!

A bunch of kids followed us all the way along the shore to the hotel. We ordered coffee on the veranda while we waited.

The Bupati was a stocky, middle-aged man with a missing front tooth that somehow added to his charm without detracting from his dignity. He asked if we could speak Dutch; we said no, and off we went in Indonesian.

We said we were going to Gunung Sitoli on the Celia. The Bupati said he was, too, which, in retrospect, should have surprised us, but didn't. Then he gave us a note to the District Officer in South Nias. We added this note to our letter from the Information Office in Palembang, the letter that the Information Officer at Sibolga had given us for the Information Office at Gunung Sitoli, the letter from the nun to her sister nuns and the letter from Father Johan to his sister and to the priest at Telak Dalam. We were collecting quite a stack of paper.

Back to the hotel for supper and bed. We were to sail the next morning.

While we were organizing our things, the agent's man came to tell us that the Celia might be held up awhile, but by tomorrow night we would be on our way.

Betul.

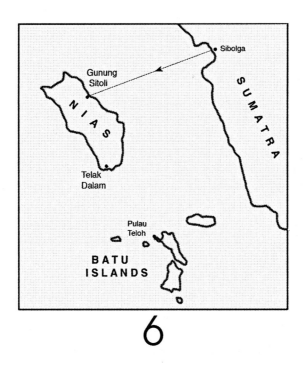

6

The Celia

Next afternoon, late, we were all on the dock.

The Governor was there to say goodbye to the Bupati.

The Police Chief was there.

The Information Officer was there, as were Mansur and the Harbormaster. There was the shipping agent, his men, some coolies, a crowd of interested onlookers and the priest who'd come down to wish us well.

The Harbormaster had a headache, so I gave him two aspirin.

The launches were gone, but there was a lighter to take us to the Celia. A lighter is a great cow of a boat with all its ribs showing on the inside. It looks like a homemade version of a lifeboat, except without any floor or seats, and it's much larger. Lighters have no power of their own. They depend on oars or tows from power-driven craft. Lighters are used to load copra.

The Customs man came to check us out. One goes through Customs to cross a street in this country.

We stood on the dock for about a half hour. Then all of us bound for the Celia got into the lighter.

Another half hour passed.

We arranged our baggage on the floor of the lighter. Some people stood on the ribs at the side, some sat on their baggage, some sat up on the prow, some stood on the floor where they couldn't see over the sides, and one got seasick. Every once in a while, a motorized sampan would chug by and everybody would scream for it to give us a tow, but they were all going home to supper.

A man on the prow had a pole, so he pushed us out from the dock just to do something, and poled us around for a while. Someone said the sunset was going to be pretty. We poled back to the dock and tied up. The man with the pole put his pole up on the dock.

Tied next to the dock was a wee little dinghy, and in the back of the dinghy was an Evinrude Big Twin outboard without its cover. Two men were working on it. One had a red scarf and no shirt. The other had a shirt and no hat. The bareheaded man was telling the red scarved man what to do. Every once in awhile, the motor would cough and quiver all over, and everyone would cheer. Then the motor would go back to sleep, and everybody would moan. Finally the motor caught, and amid the plaudits of the crowd, the dinghy limped over to the side of our lighter. In jubilation, our prow man pushed off, and we started for the ship. Then the dinghy's motor died, and we were stranded in the surf with no pole. There was excitement as we drifted closer to the rocks.

A fellow on the dock threw the pole in the water and dove in after it with all his clothes on. He grabbed the pole, swam to the lighter, and we poled around the harbor some more.

It was a lovely sunset. The moon was big and brilliant.

The little motor kept coughing and not starting. Bob whispered that he thought he knew the trouble.

"Why don't you tell them?"

"I think they're having fun," said Bob.

The moon misted over, and there was a drizzle of rain.

The motor caught again, found its voice and sounded quite sure of itself. The dingy did a couple of cocky little circles and headed for our lighter where it crashed head-on, directly amidships.

The motor coughed and died.

The rest was falling action. They revived the motor once again, lashed on to the lighter and slowly nudged us out to the Celia, like a puppy pushing a hippopotamus.

The next act developed quickly. We had watched the coolies climb on board, and were seeing to our own precious baggage when it started.

The Captain stood on the upper deck. The veins in the side of his forehead were blue and prominent, his voice harsh with fury. He was trying to talk to the agent's man in English because he didn't know any Indonesian. The agent's man didn't speak English any better than the Captain, but he could guess the meaning of "liar" and "dirty crook" from the Captain's expression. Beside them, stony faced, stood the Bupati.

Our Indonesian wasn't the best, but we volunteered to help if help was needed.

We were told that, because we had been accepted as passengers, the agent had tried to put on twenty passengers of his own.

We asked the agent if this was true.

He said it was only partially true. He had put on only five passengers, the Bupati and his staff, because the government boat was out of order and they had to get back. The rest of the people were coolies. They were there to load copra.

We relayed this to the Captain who gestured disdainfully to the Bupati and said, "They're all lying."

We gulped and said that this man was the Bupati of Nias.

"So what?" was the essence of the Captain's reply.

We explained that a bupati was like a governor, and that if the Captain expected to work around Nias and the Batu Islands, he'd better be in the Bupati's good graces, as the Bupati controlled everything in the area.

The Captain muttered that all of them were liars and then said that everyone had to get off except the Bupati and us.

Collette appeared and nervously asked us if we wouldn't like to come down for dinner. Thanks, but not yet. She asked if we would like a drink. We accepted some orange soda, but noticed that none was offered to the Bupati!

Worse and worse!

The Bupati went down to the lower deck.

We started to follow, but were stopped. We were supposed to eat with the Captain. Collette led us to the little dining room, and we were treated to a dissertation on the superiority of the white race and how, in Indo-China, they knew how to deal with these people. The Captain showed us his bruised hand and told how he had sprained it getting a crew member to admit he'd stolen something.

He sent one of his crewmembers to pick up a bottle of wine that had been on the table upstairs.

The crewmember came back to say that it was gone.

The Captain exploded again, and asked us how we could abide to live in a country with such awful people! He said that the wine had been stolen by one of the Bupati's men up on deck. Bob and I looked at each other. The Bupati's men were probably Moslems, and Moslems don't drink. The bottle had likely been taken by the Captain's own crew. In rapid and complicated English with much slang and a Southern accent that we didn't think Collette would understand, Bob and I made a decision.

Bob excused himself and went to find the Bupati, while I attempted to explain that if we were causing trouble by going as passengers on his ship, then we had best disembark.

This was not acceptable.

I went on to say that perhaps the Captain didn't understand that we were traveling under papers issued by the Indonesian government.

What did that have to do with it?

"You may not have to live here," I said, "but we do."

No response.

I used our final argument. "Those are our friends back there."

This got a response. The Captain did not see how one could be a friend to an Indonesian.

Bob came back. He'd found out that everyone was leaving the ship, including the Bupati.

The Captain sat back, astonished.

"But I told him he could stay."

"He doesn't think he should," said Bob.

"My God, why?"

"He says," Bob went on, "that they are his children, and he will stay with them."

The Captain raised his eyes to the ceiling. "I will never understand these people," he said, "I told him he could stay."

At this point, the Bupati appeared. Using us to translate, he said that he was leaving. The Captain got red in the face.

The Bupati smiled at us. "Quick to anger," he said in Indonesian, "Not good!"

Bob said that we would go, too.

The Bupati shook his head. We already had our things on board, and everyone understood that we were willing to leave. But if we left, the Captain would only get angrier. The Bupati would see us on Nias.

"Good evening." He bowed to the Captain and left.

The Captain sputtered in perplexed fury, then took out his spite on his fish.

Have you ever tried vinegar on fried eggs? It's wonderful!

It was too late to sail that night. The Captain said we could use two folding cots that were leaning up against the cabin wall. We opened them, spread our blankets, and settled in.

Late that night, a Vietnamese sailor woke us up. He was the Celia's First Officer. He was babbling excitedly in French and Vietnamese, neither of which we understood, but we got the drift in gestures. The cots belonged to him.

Okay. We had expected to sleep on the deck anyhow. We moved our blankets and went back to sleep.

The next morning, the Captain turned up while our blankets were still on the floor. He was furious. He made the First Officer apologize to us, and said a great deal more on the nature of the darker races. We suffered through that with our coffee, and then sat back to wait for the harbor-clearance papers to come through.

Noon came, and more of Collette's cooking. She was apologetic. The ship's cook had quit in Penang, she didn't know why, and for some reason they had been unable to hire another one. She served beans cooked with eggs and tomatoes. Delicious!

The sun was well past the meridian when a launch pulled out from shore. Five minutes later, the Harbormaster, resplendent in white and gold, came on board carrying a large briefcase.

He pulled out the clearance papers for the Celia. He had questions about the number of men in the crew. He checked every record carefully, and apologized profusely because the agent had been so wrong about the passengers. He waxed flowery.

The Captain kept looking at his watch.

The Harbormaster took histories of everybody in the crew, and the Captain and his wife as well. He was charming and verbose. I was so fascinated that I jumped when Bob nudged me and gestured with his thumb out to port.

From behind an island, appeared a gleaming white ship, slim as a shark and going like mad. It was the mail boat! The repairmen must have worked all night!

The Harbormaster cleared the Celia. He saluted the Captain and shook hands with us. As he held my hand, he gave a large wink. Then, at his most dignified, he returned to his launch.

We lifted anchor.

We started with a slight advantage to the white vessel, but that didn't last long. The Celia wasn't built for speed.

We reached Gunung Sitoli in the morning. We left most of our stuff on the Celia and, with several crewmembers, piled into the dingy to go to shore. As we pulled up to the jetty, a wave hit our boat and it gave a great lurch. One of the men toppled into the water, while I and my camera landed with an undignified bump on a bunch of dirty rags on the floor.

I got to my feet, brushed off my pedal pushers and looked up. The Bupati of Nias, fresh and rested after a good night's sleep, was waiting on the dock to welcome us to Nias. Not South Nias, but that didn't bother us.

Yet.

7

Gunung Sitoli

Gunung Sitoli is the capital of Nias. It a sleepy harbor town, nestled in hills overlooking a palm-fringed beach. The government buildings lie on a broad green meadow in the middle. We learned later that the beauty of Nias covers a malaria-ridden, undernourished population, but our first look was all lovely.

The first thing we did, after reporting to the police and the Information Office, was to go the KPM office to confirm our return booking.

The KPM agent was a pudgy entrepreneur named Mr. Ong. He was deliriously eager to be of service, but had bad news. The KPM ship was a week late, and might be even later by the time it reached Nias. And it wasn't stopping in South Nias after all. Why? Because the Celia was getting there first and would pick up all the copra.

Were any other vessels going from South Nias to Padang?

No.

From South Nias to Sibolga?

No.

From Gunung Sitoli to Sibolga?

No, except for the mail boat that would sail the same day as the KPM boat. And, if we went back to Sibolga, we'd have to take another bus from Sibolga back to Padang and lose two days more.

After all our trouble to get to Nias, we were stuck on Nias. And we weren't even at Bawa Matalua yet!

Mr. Ong wanted badly to help. Seemed that he also ran a travel agency. We said we'd like to hear his suggestions, but first we had to let our company know where we were, and that we'd be late getting home. Mr. Ong gave us directions to the telegraph office.

While we waited in line on the dirt path, Bob composed a message. He said where we were, and explained that the only transportation that we could conceivably take, other than the tardy KPM ship, would be a coaster, and that we had been advised that, in the rainy season, coasters were likely to sink. He added that he would take the risk if the company asked him to. Chuckling, he handed in his wire.

We went back to the KLM office. Now Mr. Ong was wearing his travel agency hat. He looked serious. If we thought it would be simple to get from Gunung Sitoli to Bawa Matalua, that all we had to do was run down the coast, we were wrong. The road was bad, and the sea route was so dangerous in the rainy season even native craft wouldn't risk it. There was only one ship going to South Nias in the foreseeable future. The Celia.

We groaned.

And even the Celia wasn't going directly to South Nias, because she had to go to the Batu Islands first.

But…Mr. Ong reached for another hat…there might be another way. He had the government contract to maintain the roads, so he knew how bad they were, but he had a special land rover jeep that might be able to make the trip. It would be expensive. He would have to pay the driver and mechanic for the trip down and back, and for all the time we were there. And there was the fuel, and possibly repairs. All told, the round trip couldn't be done for less than 3,000 rupiahs.

3,000 rupiahs! That was more than our entire trip had cost so far!

Bob pulled out a pencil. He added up the price of gas, pay and food for the driver and mechanic, wear and tear on the jeep, doubled the sum, and offered 1,000 rupiahs.

Mr. Ong was sadly shaking his head when the Information Officer turned up. He said that the hospital might have a jeep. We broke off negotiations and went to find out.

The hospital was built around an open court. Milling around, sitting on the edges of the porch, on benches, on the ground, were patients in faded kains, in rags, in almost nothing, holding babies at their breasts, nursing open sores, rickets, blindness; the sick, the halt, the lame, people who coughed, people who bled, people who wept.

The Information Officer asked a neat, white-clad Indonesian nurse where the doctor was.

She said he was out on a call. Someone else said no, he'd come back and was operating. Someone else said the operation was over, and he'd gone back to his house for a short rest. We went to his house. The house obviously doubled as an office. A nurse offered us coffee and made conversation while we waited.

The nurse told us there are two Dr. Thompsons, man and wife. He is a surgeon. She is an obstetrician and pediatrician. They had been Lutheran missionaries in Nias before the Japanese took Indonesia. They were incarcerated, and eventually sent back to their native Germany.

After Independence, the new government tried to send an Indonesian doctor to Nias, but the people wouldn't have it.

"We didn't want another doctor." said the nurse, "We wanted Dr. Thompsons only."

So the Thompsons returned to Nias as government employees. But they put all of their government salaries back into the hospital.

The Thompsons had the sun-browned leanness of people who'd worked long in the tropics. When we saw them, we guessed why they empathized with the halt and the lame. Dr. Thompson has something wrong with one eye. His wife has a withered arm. They, too, are the halt and the lame.

Mrs. Thompson excused herself to go back to the hospital, while Doctor Thompson sat down with a cup of coffee. What did we want?

We wanted to go to Bawa Matalua.

He froze, his cup halfway to his mouth.

We told him about Mr. Ong and his land rover. We asked if he had any suggestions.

Dr. Thompson said that the hospital had a jeep, but it was broken. So was their boat. We probably wouldn't like south Nias. When people wanted to go to there, he discouraged them. "They're different," he said. He didn't explain how. He stood up, said he was going back to the hospital, and left.

"I know he's a hero," said Bob, "But does he have to be so rude?"

It was time to see the Bupati.

The Bupati got Mr. Ong to cut his price. It was still more than we could afford. We thanked him and went back to the Information Office.

This Information Officer turned out to be an amateur photographer. He was interested in our equipment. When we told him what we were using, he looked dubious.

"How will you run your tape recorder without electric power?" he asked.

Bob said we had an inverter. We could run our recorder off a car battery.

"But they don't have any cars."

Bob and I looked at each other. We'd never even thought of that! Of course if we took the landrover, we would have a battery. We told this to the Information Officer.

"You can't drive from Telak Dalam to Bawa Matalua," he said. "No road. But I have a car battery you can use."

We thanked him, and he even offered to donate gasoline to Mr. Ong for our trip.

Bob and I excused ourselves and switched to English to discuss our situation.

We were more than a week into a two-week leave and we hadn't even gotten where we wanted to go. And we couldn't go back, even if we wanted to. No boat.

"How are we doing on money?"

Bob took out the pencil again. The Martimbang bus had been a bargain, and so had the hotel in Sibolga, but they hadn't been free. We hadn't expected to pay for so many days' food. Every day we delayed cost us more, and the KPM boat was at least a week late!

We certainly couldn't afford that car!

Maybe we should grit our teeth and take the Celia's detour through the Batu Islands. It would only be a day or two.

"What's copra?"

"Dried coconut."

So we would spend a day or two watching a ship load dried coconut. The Batu Islands might be pretty. We'd still have some time in South Nias. But how would we get back to Gunung Sitoli?

Then Bob had a brainstorm. What if we didn't keep the landrover for all the time we were in Telak Dalam? What if it just came down and picked us up? Could we afford that?

We went back to see Mr. Ong. Mr. Ong said he would be losing a lot of money our way and the only reason he agreed was because he liked us.

Bob went back to the Information Office, said our thanks, and hoisted the battery. Now, only our feelings about the Captain and the brotherhood of man stood between us and South Nias.

We returned to the harbor.

A broken jetty stretched like a twisted finger out into the deep blue water of the Gunung Sitoli Harbor. We walked out on it and sat down to wait for the Celia's dinghy.

A lighter was riding on heavy waves, while a swarm of coolies walked out into the surf, shoulder high, to put boxes and bundles on their heads and wade them back to shore. Every once in a while, a big wave would go completely over them. They held their burdens up as high as they could and laughed and laughed. We saw a package of schoolbooks split open. The books floated all over the harbor with the coolies after them. More laughter. Great sport!

We saw the Celia's dingy dancing around on the waves. A man had the engine up and its cover off. He would disappear behind a wave then reappear on the top of the next wave, still working.

We hired a "little motorboat".

Our "little motorboat" was a large sampan with a roofed end. The roof was flat so people could ride up there. Under the roof were a greasy, antiquated diesel engine and a crew of three. One man ran the engine, one waited with a screw-driver, and the third was a small boy with a pail. A tin pipe went from the side of the vessel down to the engine. On top of this was a funnel. The small boy's job was to hoist buckets of water from the sea and pour them through the funnel to water-cool the engine. Bob and I crawled down into this engine room, but we didn't stay long. When the boat took off, the smoke and the smell drove us out into the open, where we stood holding on to the edge until we reached the Celia.

The Captain and his wife greeted us happily. That night, over herbed fish braised in butter, we learned how America had lost Indochina for the French. Only the French, we were told, understood that those people were meant to be slaves, and had to be beaten to keep them in line. Education just made trouble. They were happier without it. But we unenlightened Americans went in and told the people that they should go to school, so they rebelled. Then the American government smuggled in millions of dollars worth of arms for the express purpose of defeating the French.

The Captain wanted to know why our government was so anti-French?

We couldn't tell the Captain why our government was anti-French, because we didn't believe it was, but we could have told him why we were becoming anti one French captain.

The Captain couldn't understand why we were traveling around the way we were, as there was nothing on these islands, absolutely nothing. He hadn't both-ered to learn the language because all you had to do was to shout at the natives and point. He never went ashore. He went fishing, and advised us to do the same. The Captain said, glumly, that he thought it would take at least six days on Pulau Teloh to load, as they were lazy bums. Then he gave us his views on why the Martians had brought their flying saucers and were watching the Earth, and Bob beat him in three games of chess out of spite, and we went to bed.

That night the hammock broke.

Bob and I lay awake and listened to the swish of the water as we ploughed our way along under the stars. This deck passage business really has something to be said for it! You get the breeze. You can watch the horizon rolling slowly up and down with the movement of the ship. You can watch the phosphorus in the water and the schools of flying fish. The moon flirts with you under and out of the clouds like a baby playing peek-a-boo. And there are no walls. Bob and I had spent the first night down on the deck itself, where we could feel the vibration of the ship lulling us asleep.

But white people aren't supposed to sleep on decks like natives, so when we refused to use the First Officer's cot, the Captain had dug up a couple of hammocks that he slung, with great effort, from the bracings of the deck canopy. Then he rigged a rope to hold the gate closed to protect us from those ruffians downstairs who might slit our throats, and told us where we could find the key to the icebox, which was secured by an enormous padlock.

I never was fond of hammocks because, if you sink far enough into them to not fall out, you can't move and must lie like a patient under restraint, with your arms either crossed on your breast or losing circulation at your sides. Your head flops forward, and your feet rest somewhat higher. I finally fell asleep, but woke feeling that I would never move again.

There was a noise like that of a small boy running along a fence with a stick. If it were possible to sit upright in a hammock, I would have. The noise repeated itself. Bob dumped himself out and examined his hammock. The sound had been the strands breaking. His hammock was hanging by a hair. Bob pushed on the last rope and it broke.

We spread our blankets on the deck. With the rumble of the engine under us and moonlight glistening on our wake, we slept like babies.

We woke to the deep rattle of a falling anchor.

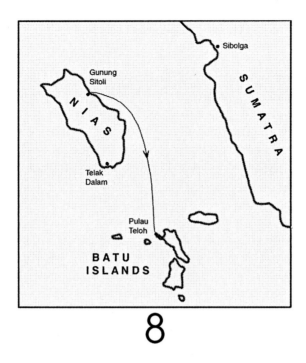

8

The Copra Islands

It rained on our first morning at Palau Teloh. The Captain and Collette didn't go fishing because the shipping agent was mad at the Captain and wouldn't use his dingy to push the lifeboat out to the fishing grounds. There was a mix-up about landing. The Customs man wanted to see our papers. We gave him our letter to the Information Office, and he set off for shore while we set about doing our laundry and catching up on our notes.

Did I tell you that there was a parrot in the shower? The Celia housed several animals. There were a lot of chickens, two of which fluttered overboard and drowned on the trip. The rest gave eggs that Collette carefully dated and put in the refrigerator. There were two little civet cats that Collette was trying to house-break, but they wouldn't cooperate. There were two monkeys in crew's quarters, and a lot of fish.

The shower didn't work because the engine was off, but if I got there soon enough, I could catch a trickle.

The john didn't work either. We solved this with buckets, and I suspect that the Vietnamese sailor who left clothes soaking in the washroom wondered why all his nice soapy water had evaporated, leaving old soggy cloth at the bottom of the pail. Maybe he noticed the soapsuds in the commode and figured it out. If he didn't, the parrot did. It screeched like mad when we pilfered that water. It also screeched when we showered. It's disconcerting to hear rude comments when one stands in a helpless state of undress. That parrot was well-grounded in the facts of life.

In the afternoon, the sun came out. The Captain pulled out some oars and invited us to go fishing with him. We thanked him, but declined. Then the shipping agent came back with his dinghy and our papers and offered to take us ashore. We accepted.

In sunlight, Pulau Teloh looks like a south sea travel poster. The shore is a half moon of palm trees curving over white sand. The water is blue as blue, shading from light turquoise near land to glistening sapphire in deeper water. Farther out, a smaller island forms a deep green breakwater.

Outrigger canoes were scattered like petals across the water, and, near the shore, we saw the swift winging of a fisherman's net. Gulls soared above us, and every once in a while a school of flying fish rose, glittered against the sun, and slipped back into the water.

We climbed out of the dinghy onto the jetty and followed the shipping agent to the Customs shed where we had to show our passports and fill out immigration forms. Sometimes this happens. Not all the islands have accepted unity. Back in Palembang, some workers from Java expect overseas pay.

After Customs, we followed the patut routine. First, call on the police. Then report to the Information Office. Then call on the highest official. On Pulau Teloh, this was a chamat.

The Chief of Police was huge. He looked as if he could tear you apart with his bare hands. He examined our passports and handed them back.

"Bet they don't have much crime here," Bob whispered after we bowed our goodbyes.

"I'm glad he was smiling," I said.

The Information Officer was expecting us. He was the personification of a noble Polynesian, with his long hair and his gleaming white teeth set in a wide, perfectly-formed mouth.

"I take you to the Chamat." He led us out into the sunlight.

At first sight, the town of Pulau Teloh seems to consist only of the jetty, the Customs shed, a warehouse and a town with just one street. Pressing in from all sides are acre after acre of coconut trees. Unless you have seen really old coconut trees, you can't conceive how majestic they are, or how clear and alive their fronds look with sun gleaming through them.

The Information Officer told us he was born on Pulau Teloh and went to high school in Gunung Sitoli. With his high school certificate, he got a government job back on Pulau Teloh. He didn't want to live anywhere else.

He pointed out the new school.

The Indonesian Government is building its school system three years at a time. When the children in a village have been educated to grade six, they open grades seven, eight, and nine. When three more years have passed, maybe they can staff a high school. The system feeds back teachers as literacy grows. The villages build new schools as their students progress. The program is still in the stumbling stage, but it is moving, and although there is a lack of books and materials, there is no lack of enthusiasm and will.

"Watch out!" We moved aside to make way for a cart pushed by eight or ten straining coolies.

"Copra," The Information Officer began doing his job. "Pulau Teloh is the heart of the copra trade. Some people call us the 'Copra Islands' because this is where the trade began. He said that Pulau Teloh's copra is shipped from the Batu Islands to Malaya and Singapore where the oil is refined. Copra oil is not "palm oil". Palm oil comes from another kind of tree, and is used for margarine and cooking oil. Copra oil is a base for soap.

So that was why the islands were known as the Copra Islands, but why, we wondered, were they named the Batu Islands? "Batu" means "stone."

The Information Officer wasn't sure. Maybe it came from the old stone things in the village.

Old stone things?

The Chamat was a pudgy man, wearing the whitest of white shirts and a neat black fez. We were welcome. What were we doing on his island?

We said that we were trying to get to Bawa Matalua to take pictures of the Nias big house and, we hoped, some dances. But we had difficulties. We told him how we happened to be on the Celia, and what a happy surprise it was to discover his lovely island.

He sat straighter. "Pulau Teloh has Nias culture, too," he said proudly. He added that they didn't have the costumes for the dances, but they knew the old songs. The children learned the dances in school. If we wanted, he could close the school for a day so the children could dance for us.

That would be wonderful!.

Would we like to see the village?

Village? Yes, indeed!

Good. We could see the village the next day, but they would need another day to set things up with the school. Anything else?

Yes. Where could we get something to eat?

It took a while to convince the Information Officer that we liked Indonesian food. He'd heard that white people didn't like hot foods. After we assured him that we did, he and the Chamat took us to a restaurant with a plank floor and a corrugated iron roof and wonderful food.

There's something about eating together that breaks the ice. The Chamat apologized for delaying us on the ship. He hadn't seen our letter yet and he'd heard bad things about the Captain. He didn't want a "colonial" on the island because it might cause trouble.

We understood. The Captain was quick to anger. He had been good to us, but he had been rude to everyone else, so we preferred to stay away from the ship as much as possible because, if things came to a head, we didn't want to be in the middle.

The Chamat nodded. He had given orders that the Captain and his wife were not to land. We, however, had the freedom of the island.

The freedom of the island! We spent the afternoon strutting around looking for good pictures to take the next day. Then we went back to the ship.

We were testing a camera when the Captain and his wife came back from fishing. They wanted to know what we were doing.

We told them there was a village we were going to photograph.

The Captain said he thought he'd come along!

You could hear the wind.

Bob quickly said that it was just an old village, way out in the jungle, at the same time that I said we would have to have the Chamat's permission.

The Captain waved his hand, as if brushing off a fly. We shouldn't worry about him. It was a public road, and anybody could walk down it. What could a native chief do about that? He'd never dreamed there could be anything worth photographing on such an insignificant island. Now that he knew, he'd come along. He liked to take pictures.

We thought of the huge Chief of Police.

We thought of the pistols in the belts, of the guards in the Customs shed.

The veins showed in the Captain's temple. What was wrong? Wasn't he good enough to come ashore with us?

We tried to explain that we were guests ourselves. We would have to have permission to bring more guests.

That wouldn't do, said the Captain. No colored man had to give the Captain permission to go anywhere. Obviously, we didn't want his company. The trouble, he announced with wringing bitterness, was that he had assumed that Americans were like Englishmen. He was obviously wrong. With this scathing comment, he stalked off to bed. Collette gave us an apologetic glance as she started after him.

We arranged our blankets and debated what we could have done differently. If we'd told the Captain that he wasn't allowed on shore, he might have charged in just to prove that nobody could order him around. What would have happened then? We decided that, although the Captain would never understand our reasoning, we had done him a favor.

The Copra Trade

9

An Amazing Day

The next day, the shipping agent towed the Captain out to the fishing grounds. Then he came back and took us to shore, where the Chamat and the Police Chief were waiting.

The village was a twenty-minute walk. We started to carry our equipment, but the Chamat wouldn't let us. He had convened a safari of porters for our cameras, tripod, tape recorder, battery and gadget bag. One man even offered to carry my purse.

Bob was worried about the fellow who was carrying the battery. He looked awfully little, but the Chamat wouldn't let Bob take it. So we started off. The little fellow with the big battery was at the end of the procession.

We went through acres of coconut trees. We crossed little brooks. Every once in a while, we walked by the sea. We passed palm-thatched houses and children in ragged kains or nothing at all. They giggled and waved at us.

We stopped to take a picture of a man shinnying up a huge coconut tree, his machete gleaming in one hand, his head bound in a bright kerchief, his heels tied together for easier traction. He climbed faster when he saw our cameras.

We took a picture of a rickety shed where copra was drying on a bamboo rack over deep coals. Smoke billowed through the brittle palm-frond roof, and I wondered what a New York fire inspector would say about that.

After about half an hour, we came to a cleared space and a stone bench, where the Chamat suggested we stop and rest.

To our right, a sloping path wandered beneath banyan trees and palm trees down to the beach and the sea. Several little boys ran past us to the shore and jumped into the surf to play.

After a few minutes, the Chamat stood up and led us away from the sea. Two stone pillars guarded the end of the path. We walked past them into a central clearing ringed by low palm-thatched houses. On one side was a well. On the other, a palm-thatched balai sheltered two overturned outriggers.

Directly ahead of us stood a real Nias chief's house!

There were the huge logs placed in a V to support the raised floor. There was the stone courtyard and the carved stone throne for the chief and the spirits to sit. And there was the steep roof, sloping up to several times the height of the facade. The roof was palm-thatched except for a tiny fringe of corrugated iron at the front.

The Chamat apologized for the thatch. Pulau Teloh, he said, was too poor to buy corrugated iron. So we took pictures of what we learned later was the only Nias chief's house with an original palm-thatched roof.

We were packing our cameras when we heard an excited babble of voices, and a boy ran up gesticulating wildly. "The battery, the battery, broken!"

Bob ran back to check. Sure enough, the little man had tripped and dropped the battery. Battery acid seeped out on the stone. The man had disappeared. Everyone eyed us apprehensively, but we were worried more about the acid than the battery. The children were barefoot.

We weren't angry?

No. But quick, wipe up the acid before someone gets hurt.

The Chamat sent for another battery. Where would he get one? There is no electricity on Pulau Teloh. We suspect that he commandeered a battery off one of the Chinese coasters riding in the harbor.

We had to wait. Where? Why in the chief's house, of course.

I felt a shiver of excitement.

Nias chief's houses were built to show the power of the chief. The higher the roof, the greater the chief. This house was raised on pillars and its roof was about 70 to 80 feet high. The front of the house jutted out like the aft of a galleon and was latticed so that one could look directly down onto the stone porch below. What a fine place from which to throw weapons down at attackers! The floor was well above our heads and supported by a criss-cross labyrinth of huge logs. To enter, we went to the side, climbed a narrow wooden stair wedged between logs, and walked in under the house on a wooden walkway. Turning right, we faced an even larger stair.

This was the only entrance; here, deep in the dark bowels of the understructure.

This house would be impregnable to primitive weapons! From this chaos of bracing logs, a man could stand off a small army. We climbed the hidden stair and turned left into the main hall which was an immense square room with a raised dais extending all the way across the front. The windows were small slits in the walls. This house was a fortress as well as a meeting place.

Above us another jumble of logs crossed, this way and that, until they vanished into the shadows under the eaves far above. A few great polished pillars extended up from the floor. One in particular caught my attention. About ten feet up was a carved circular plate-like ledge, elaborately decorated underneath.

I asked its purpose. I was told that it was where people used to put meat. This didn't seem practical to me. Then a shiver ran up my spine as I remembered that the Niha collected heads.

I looked away from the ledge and around the room. There were many smaller ledges, all elaborately carved, and all empty. One depicted a carved throne with a canopy. Others had symbols carved on the walls above them. I knew from Loeb's *Sumatra* what they must be. The old people had ceremonies by which they captured the spirit of a dead or dying person. They housed these spirits in wooden or stone statues, and put the statues up in places of honor so the spirit could remain in its home.

The people were Christian now. The idols were gone, but their empty pedestals remained.

I looked up, again.

Strung under the massive cross pieces were great necklaces of animal skulls. These were the skulls of pigs killed for feasts given by the chief, and placed up there as permanent reminders of his greatness.

The old Niha kept slaves. Skilled slaves built these houses. The more skilled the slaves, the greater the house. When the house was finished, it was possible for the slaves to build another better house for somebody else, so they had to be done away with. But, because they must love their own work, there was no reason why their spirits shouldn't guard it. Artisan slaves were split and buried under the front and the back of the house. I don't mean that if you had a dozen slaves, you buried six in the front and six in the back. No, you buried twelve halves in the front and twelve halves in the back.

When all these spirit protectors were in place, there was one last ritual to perform. You had to remove any bad spirits that might still be in the house. To do this, pigs were hoisted to the top of the house and rolled down the roof. The bad spirits leaped out the windows to get the meat. Then the priests inside pulled in the ropes and slammed the windows shut. The house was safe. I remembered that the old Niha had referred to themselves as "the pigs of God".

I saw something that I didn't recognize hanging on the wall above the chief's chair. It looked like an easel. What symbolic meaning could it have? I asked.

The Chamat answered. The main room was no longer used for ceremonies. Now, it was the schoolroom for the adult literacy program. That was the easel for their blackboard.

A door opened. Everybody stood up, as into the room came a very old man, trying to walk independently of his two attendants. With great dignity, he shuffled across the floor, his seamed face pale with sickness, but his old eyes bright. He nodded his welcome, but did not smile. A Nias chief does not have to smile.

Two young women brought in coconuts with their tops cut off. The old chief gestured for us to refresh ourselves.

Next, the old chief gave a speech of welcome, not once smiling, his dark eyes moving from Bob's to mine. His voice was thin but firm. He didn't speak Indonesian, so the Chamat translated his words. We whispered that we would love to take a picture of him, but the Chamat said that was not possible. The old man was seriously ill. He had only gotten up to welcome us to his house.

The chief sipped a little coconut water, and then with a slight smile, allowed his attendant to help him out of his chair. They shuffled into the darkness.

We watched him disappear. Had he been part of the old culture? Had he taken heads?

Now he sponsored an adult education class in his house.

From the looks around the table, we knew the chief was revered, and we knew he was dying.

We went back down the dark stairway and out into the sun.

Several men were gathered around the stone thrones, waiting to sing the old songs.

The first song described the way the prow of a small boat rides up and down in the water, and how nice it is to fish. You'd never know it to hear it. Niha singing is totally nasal, and goes on and on in a monotonous rhythm. We were glad to record it, but we think we know why the old songs are being forgotten.

We recorded two more songs before we said thanks to the singers, to our hosts, and to one small boy whom we had been using as an actor in a few shots. He puffed up his thin chest, said that now he was a film star, and scampered off.

We packed up with a sense of satisfaction. We had stumbled on a beautiful place, and we had done what we could to record it.

We thought we were through, but we were wrong. There is so much more to tell about that amazing day!

On the way back, we passed a little unpainted frame building with people crowded on its porch. We caught sight of what looked like a nurse's uniform. Surprised, we asked about it.

"That is our polyclinic."

Did they have a doctor?

No, but they had two nurses from Doctor Thompson's hospital in Gunung Sitoli.

What happens if someone needs a doctor?

Then they must go to Gunung Sitoli, or wait until Dr. Thompson comes to Pulau Teloh.

Goodness, we thought, when does he find the time?

We stopped at an open stall for lunch. We had rice, eggs, and tea. No fresh vegetables.

"Can't vegetables grow here?"

"Yes. And Dr. Thompson says we should grow them. But it's hard. The soil is mostly sand and coral. Some people eat the tops of rice or potato plants, and there's always coconut and lots of fish. But fresh fruits and vegetables must be imported."

No wonder there were so many skin disorders and rickets cases!

As we left the restaurant, we heard a buzzing sound like a swarm of insects. We tried to locate it, but it wasn't until we looked up that we saw several brightly colored kites dancing against the clouds. We had heard about singing kites. They are found all through central Sumatra and even on Java, but this is the first time we had seen them.

A man down the road was attaching a tail to a kite. We went to watch. He showed us the thin bamboo strip that stretches across the top and vibrates in the wind. Bob got dizzy taking pictures of kites swooping around in the sky.

Then I rode in an outrigger canoe.

A Pulau Teloh canoe is hollowed out of a tree trunk. A floor is added a couple of inches below the rail and notches are carved to hold the outrigger which is an oblong frame of bamboo with heavy rattan logs lashed onto both ends and a hole in the center to hold a mast because the boat can be either rowed or sailed. The sail is an irregular rectangle something like the mainsail on a gaff rig. It is kept wrapped on the boom when not in use.

Three men manned our outrigger. The Information Officer helped carry the boom from the house to the shore. His dignity had vanished with his shirt. His teeth gleamed white as he laughed. He inserted one end of the boom into a hole in the mast. A rope was run up the mast and the upper spar raised, pulling the sail up with it. Turned out our Information Officer was the best sailor on the island.

I took one camera with me, while Bob photographed from shore with the other. I climbed on board, knelt down in the center, and we took off. The Information Officer sat by the tiller at the stern, one sailor stood at the mast, and one sat at the prow with the wind blowing his dark hair.

You can't imagine from watching, just how fast these little craft are. The prow goes up and down with the waves, but the outriggers keep you steady side to side. I watched the outriggers skimming along on either side of me, while above me the sail rose tautly to the sky.

In no time at all, we had reached the islands opposite and were turning back. I could have stayed out all day! The information Officer looked at me with a proud smile, as though I were a child who had been presented with an ice cream cone. Too soon, the sailors changed the angle of sail. We drifted in to shore and nestled snugly onto the beach. I climbed out and pushed back my hair.

Time for tea.

We stopped in one of the few houses in town that had a toilet. It belonged to a Chinese merchant. He wasn't there, but his wives were. All three of them. We were introduced and learned that not only were we expected for tea, we were expected to take a bath! It seems that in Niha country, baths always come before supper.

Remembering my Indonesian manners, I suggested that Bob bathe first. He went happily down the hall, and I was left with the ladies. They eyed me like Cinderella's stepsisters might have eyed the prince.

I was offered lemonade which I accepted without thinking, and then was aghast when I realized it was made with fresh water. I pretended to sip as I visualized all the little bacteria swimming around in the glass.

The ladies asked me if I had any children, and I said not yet, which dried up that source of conversation. Then they asked me where I had bought my skirt.

I said I had made it.

Oh. Did I have any patterns?

Yes.

Would I send them to them?

(Gasp) I'd see.

Did I have a fashion book?

No.

Could I get one?

(Smaller gasp. I was catching on.) Maybe.

Would I send one to them?

Maybe.

Did I know what a meat grinder was?

Yes.

Would I buy one for them?

Maybe. (This could turn out to be the most expensive bath in history.)

How about the clothes I was wearing?

They told me how poor they were. They only had a palm-thatched roof on their servants' quarters and they yearned for corrugated iron. Three sad pairs of eyes turned to me.

Bob came back, clean, and I escaped to the bath,

Or did I? While I stood there by the big stone cistern washing myself down with buckets of water, each wife took her turn.

"Soap?"

I already had some. She took a good look and left.

Towel?

I had one. She looked and left.

The third couldn't think of a reason to be there, so she showed me how faded her dress was. I said I thought it was pretty. She giggled girlishly, and left.

Then came the potatoes.

This potato business is embarrassing. People seem to think that Europeans eat potatoes like Indonesians eat rice, and Indonesians eat rice by piling a soup plate high with it, pouring sauce on top, eating it all, and going back for more. To eat potatoes this way, you'd have to make a meal of about five or six big Idaho baking potatoes and a little bit of gravy, and that's all. But that's what they think we want. Potatoes are imported. Potatoes are expensive. But they will cook up enough potatoes to feed a small army, then stand around proudly while you try to make a dent in the potatoes.

We hope the women enjoyed what we couldn't possibly eat.

We left them our towel.

There were a lot of people sitting on the dock. Most of our friends were there, resting after the day. They greeted us and went back to their contemplation of the darkening sky. Some children squatted nearby spitting into the water.

The Chief of Police was there. He had changed his uniform for a sarong, and he had a little boy on his lap. He was trying to clean out an open sore on the child's leg. It looked like yaws.

We asked about the child. It was his son. The sore had been there for over a month and hadn't healed. There was some sort of "injection" which could cure it, but there was none on the island.

We had some penicillin salve. We said we'd bring it the next day, and sat down to wait for the boat.

The moon was up. The water lapped comfortably at the rocks, and the stars slowly appeared.

In time, the boat came, and we rode back to the ship.

The Captain didn't have much to say to us. He went to bed.

We stood at the rail watching lights moving on shore. "Do you think they are still loading?"

"They can't be. The hatches are closed."

We watched the lights for a while.

"You know, even if we never get to Bawa Matalua, we've been in a real Nias chief's house."

"We'll get to Bawa Matalua."

"If we don't run out of money."

We went to sleep.

Next morning we were up bright and early.

We gave the salve to the Chief of Police and went with the Information Officer to the school. We passed a train of copra carts on our way.

The children danced in the schoolyard. What would the old gods have thought to see their sacred dances performed by happy children in faded school uniforms?

We taped until the recorder broke down and we had used all the film we'd brought. Then we shot with no film in the camera, so as not to disappoint.

We'd done what we could. We went back to the restaurant for lunch.

Bob dismantled the tape recorder. He wasn't sure whether the problem was in the recorder or the battery. We never did find out. When we finally got back home, it ran perfectly.

Bob concluded that the recorder was useless, and went to the beach to hunt for shells.

The water was clear and the waves came up in lazy rolls. A lot of children were playing around the dock. When they saw Bob wading in, they waded in too. Pretty soon, dozens of children were wading around looking for shells. When they found a nice one, they would dash up to Bob, show it to him, then go back and hunt some more.

Bob got hungry. He climbed up on the dock with his wet handkerchief full of lovely cat's eyes. He gave them to me. That started a fad. Soon I was surrounded by brown hands full of shells. I took shells until Bob's handkerchief bulged and my pockets were full.

We returned to the restaurant and sat down in the tiny back room. Small hands reached through the window with more shells. The manager tried to chase the children away, but we asked him to wait. We bought all of his candy, took it outside and tried to make sure that everybody got a piece. There was one piece left over.

I surveyed the crowd of breathless urchins and saw, wide-eyed at the edge of the crowd, a very little boy that I was sure hadn't been there before. I gave him the last piece. He pulled his hand from behind his back. In it was the biggest, shiniest cat's eye I've ever seen! He flashed a tiny, shy smile, thrust the shell into my hand and skittered off as fast as he could.

We were finishing our supper when the agent's man came to tell us that the Celia would sail at five o'clock.

Already?

When we first came to Pulau Teloh, the Captain predicted that we would be there six days.

The agent said we would be there two days, at the most, three.

The first day, according to the Captain, we loaded 400 bags of copra.

According to the agent it was 800.

The second day, the Captain laughed nastily and said they had only loaded 300 bags.

The agent said they had loaded 800.

The third day the agent told the Captain that they might finish loading that day.

The Captain laughed and went fishing.

We remembered the lights we'd seen on shore the night before, and Bob pointed to two coasters. If the coolies had loaded the coasters at night, all they would have had to do the next day would be to unload the copra into the Celia. We had seen the coasters nudging their way out in the morning. The Captain hadn't. He'd been fishing.

So we would sail at five. Okay.

We went down to the jetty to wait for the boat. One of the agent's men, a clown with thick glasses and a hunch-shouldered way of talking with his hands, sighed a great groaning sigh. "Our Captain," he said with mock sadness, "Our great Captain. All day he just catches fish!!" Everyone chuckled. We sat and looked into the water. I had a little flashlight, which amused everyone for a while. A sampan slipped silently up to the dock, and everyone watched the late fisherman get out and go off to supper. Even in the moonlight, you could see deep into the water and watch the fish darting around. We did that. A few people went to sleep. An hour passed and another sampan pulled up.

The shipping agent got out. The delay had been because the Captain had still been out fishing when the loading was complete. And the outboard engine was broken again. Could we take a sampan back to the Celia?

We climbed up the ladder for the last time to find the Captain and his wife placing their haul around the deck. The Captain had a strained look about him. Collette was averting her eyes.

We helped them untangle their fishing line, and looked with some consternation at their catch. There was a dark mass of kelp dripping from the table, several lumps of wet coral on the deck, and a very large and noxious looking clam slowly dying upstream from where we planned to sleep.

The Captain was in an ill humor because he was expected to sail at night, and it was impossible to navigate out of this harbor after dark because the natives had let the buoys go to ruin. But we made it with the aid of the moon and a native boat with a lantern that hovered over the danger spot so the Captain could go around it.

While the Captain was handling this maneuver, Collette managed to re-tangle the fishing line. The Captain scolded her and there was a big fight. At last, he threw us a cold, "Adieu," and stamped off to bed. Collette picked up one of the civet cats from where it was pulling off pieces of the dying clam and followed.

We lay on the trembling deck and watched the moon and the sea and the stars.

While we slept, a slimy green mess trickled down from the clam and got on our blankets. We didn't discover that until the next day.

Next stop, South Nias.

Benar! Betul! Pasti!

Pulau
Teloh

Dawn from the Deck of the Celia

Children

The Great Seashell Hunt

Friends with a Kite

Evening

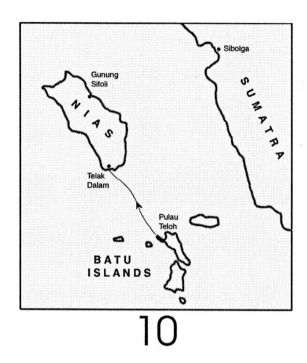

10

Telak Dalam

Early next morning we stood at the Celia's rail looking at the port of Telak Dalam. It was so small!

"Good morning." The shipping agent was below us in his dinghy. "Getting off here?"

"Yes."

Did we need a ride to shore?

Yes.

Good. He would take us. This was his home. If we wanted, we could leave our things above his father's store for safekeeping. Did we have a place to stay?

We thought we might stay at the mission.

He could take us there. He knew the sisters.

We said a polite goodbye to the Captain and Collette, handed down our things and climbed aboard.

The shipping agent helped us stow our baggage at his father's store, then shepherded us through Customs and the police to the Information Office.

The Information Officer was a slight, young Niha man who spoke Indonesian better than he read it. He struggled with our letter from Mr. Tobing back in Palembang, skipped through our letter from the Bupati, then shook our hands in welcome. When he learned that we were going to the new school to deliver the Sibolga priest's letter to his ailing sister, the Information Officer offered to take us there himself so that the shipping agent could get back to the Celia. We thanked the agent, said goodbye and turned our attention to Nias.

It took no time at all to walk through shabby little Telak Dalam and into sago fields.

In Indonesia, sago takes the place of rice when times get hard. The pulpy wood is scraped out and strained and made into a fine powder that is used as flour.

We left the sago and walked onto a brand new gravel road. We twisted up the side of a mountain until we had a lovely view of the harbor and of the wee Celia far below us,

We turned a corner, and there was a fine new wood and stone building with fresh sawdust around the front door and empty whitewash buckets against the wall.

A sweet-faced Asian nun greeted us. We gave her the letter, and she led us past the schoolrooms, up the wide fresh wood stairs to the quarters where the boarding students and the sisters lived.

She stopped the men at the entrance to the nun's quarters, and motioned me through.

Father Johan's sister lay in a room under the eaves overlooking the hills and the harbor. Above her was strung a complicated contraption of splints made from hand-hewn lumber and stone weights hung by native rope. The sister said that although they didn't have a doctor, they had a very clever lay brother who had worked in a hospital. He had a book with some diagrams of medical equipment. He had made this thing.

She wasn't sure of the extent of her injury, but what worried her most was that, after all the work to open the school, she had slipped on the first day and left them short-handed. She was afraid the authorities would recall her. She wanted to stay!

The room was dreadfully hot. I wondered how it would feel lying there, bathed in perspiration, and unable to move more than one's head and arms. But she seemed glad to see me, and the other nuns kept popping in and out, excited at having visitors.

When they heard we had brought her a letter from her brother, they got even more excited. Someone decided that, considering the special occasion, it might be all right for men to visit, too, so Bob came in with our entourage. The little Asian nun pressed us to take more and more cookies and lemonade. Sago cookies. They were good!

The Information Officer was a big help. We had three languages working, Indonesian, Dutch and Niha, and he was fluent in all three. Bob and I began to call him "Mr. Begini."

"Begini" means "it's like this" in Indonesian. Every time the Information Officer translated from another language to Indonesian, he would say, very slowly, "Begini," then he would break into such fast Indonesian that it was hard for us to keep up.

Everything was happy and relaxed until the ailing sister said that the new school was necessary because the Protestant school in Gunung Sitoli was so bad.

Bob and I exchanged looks. Should I say something? Maybe the Gunung Sitoli School really was bad. It's hard to find teachers in Indonesia. But I was a teacher in a Protestant school.

I said that I understood how hard it was to provide good teaching because I taught at the Methodist English School in Palembang. I quickly added that, although I was a Protestant, I admired the Catholic school system.

Her face fell, only very slightly, but it fell.

We excused ourselves as graciously as we could and started back down the hill.

We knew the nuns expected us to stay with the priest and had already sent him a note, but had they realized that we were not officially members of their flock? Besides, with a new school and a wounded headmistress, the father had enough on his plate without having to shepherd us. On the way down the hill, we asked Mr. Begini if there was a Protestant mission in Teluk Dalam.

He brightened. Indeed there was! There was a Lutheran mission, and he was a member. Would we like to go there?

Yes, we would, but first we should see the District Officer.

The District Officer knew our names. Someone had sent him a letter. Who had it been? He pulled open a drawer.

"The Information Office in Palembang?" Bob suggested.

"No." He closed the drawer and opened another. "Wanted help." he mumbled, "Make a good time." He ruffled through some papers.

"The Bupati?" asked Bob.

"No." He pulled out a letter, glanced at it, "Bangun Harahap."

We laughed and laughed.

The District Officer's assistant brought us tea. He was a lean young man with an unpronounceable name. When I tried to get my tongue around it, he flicked his hand toward his heart, gave a small bow and said, "My name is Peter." I was grateful for his western convenience name.

When Peter heard that we wanted to go to the Lutheran mission, his eyes lit up. He was a Protestant, too, so the District Officer sent him along, as well.

I was having second thoughts about crashing unexpectedly in on a stranger, but when Reverend Richter threw open his door and said, "Willkommen! Willkommen!" my uncertainty vanished and we gratefully entered the parsonage.

Reverend Richter was a stocky German whose schoolboy English improved as the evening went on. His wife had no English, so we talked with her in Indonesian.

The Richters had recently returned to Nias. They had a brand new house behind the old frame church, and we were their first guests.

They celebrated that fact. While Peter and Mr. Begini helped Bob pick up our things from the store, the Richters constructed a screen around the bed in the extra room, just for us. We didn't have a common language, but we got along beautifully with spotty English, elementary Indonesian, gestures and good will.

Bob and I had a few canned goods left. Among them was a large can of peach halves that Frau Richter put into her tiny kerosene refrigerator. She was very proud of that refrigerator. It couldn't have been more than four cubic feet, but for all their years before the war, they had never owned a refrigerator. We appreciated it, too. Ice water is as rare as champagne on these islands.

Before supper, Herr Richter showed us around their church and their new house. Then Frau Richter lit a kerosene lamp, led us to the back of the house and proudly showed us the new shower and bathroom that her husband had designed.

The parsonage was beside a hill, and down the hill came a stream. This was diverted by means of a split bamboo tube that ran through the wall of the washroom and emptied into a huge cistern. By swinging around a second piece of bamboo, one could pipe water over the wall and into the shower next door. Under the eaves on the other side of the shower was another cistern. This was supplied with rainwater from a series of bamboo gutters. Both cisterns had faucets at their bases.

Next to this ingenious arrangement was a closed toilet that you reached through yet another door. The spill from the cisterns went under the floor, providing constant drainage and emptying farther down into the stream, where it disappeared into the hill and didn't join anyone else's water supply.

We showered and returned for dinner.

Frau Richter served wonderful brown bread! We forgot that some Europeans eat bread and butter with a knife and fork. Everyone laughed.

Herr Richter thought the new Catholic school was a good thing. "The children won't have to go to Gunung Sitoli for high school."

He had heard about the injured nun. "She must wait for the dry season when Dr. Thompson comes. And perhaps a proper boat."

After supper, Mrs. Richter served the peaches. We protested, but she said that we were her first guests, and so we would have peaches. After we had each eaten two slices each, there were two halves left over. We insisted that they take them, but Mrs. Richter refused. She wasn't hungry, she said. So Bob ate one, and Herr Richter ate the other, but Herr Richter just ate the flesh. Then he looked questioningly at his wife. She shook her head at first, but then nodded, and he gave her the juice. She savored it like manna.

Bob says that half slice he ate will haunt him for the rest of his days.

After dinner, Reverend Richter told us about himself.

When the Japanese took Indonesia, the Richters and the Thompsons were interned, first in a Dutch camp in Indonesia that was terrible, then in a British camp in India which was comfortable. There, the Japanese administrator noticed that the Richters and the Thompsons were German allies, not Dutch enemies, and sent them home. After the war, Reverend Richter asked to be sent back to Nias.

He had a theory about why the southern Niha are different. He blamed it on the old religion. He said that the Niha are Christian now, but it's hard to break old habits of suspicion and hostility and greed. A party, or a house, or gaining status, can be more important than the community or planning for the future.

There are exceptions, he said, like the local Niha pastor who held the church together all through the occupation and the revolution, and handed it back to Reverend Richter stronger than it had been before the war.

"There are good people here," he said.

He called to the back of the house. Several people came in. We sat around the table and had a worship service in Niha. Bob and I followed as well as we could, which wasn't very well. The only thing I was sure of was the Lord's Prayer because everybody knew it by heart.

After the service, we went to bed in the brand new bedroom. It smelled of newly cut lumber. I lay on clean sheets in a real bed and thought of our day. I thought of the Celia, and the sago fields, and the new school. I thought of the injured sister who wanted so badly to stay, but whose injuries might send her back. I remembered the sweet-faced nun in Sibolga who wanted to come, but hadn't been called. I went to sleep.

11

Bawa Matalua

We had read that to get to Bawa Matalua, one has to walk for hours over a path. This is not true. You can bicycle for hours instead.

Next morning, Mr. Begini and Peter turned up with bicycles, and Mr. Begini outlined his plan for the day. He had sent a message to Bawa Matalua to let them know we were coming, but wasn't sure it had gotten there in time for anyone to make any arrangements. There were, of course, no phones.

We secured as much as we could carry on the bicycles, a day's worth of food, a change of clothes and our photographic stuff. Thank goodness we couldn't use the tape recorder or a battery! As it was, we had to leave some things at Reverend Richter's house.

Off we went down a rolling path beside the sea. Every once in a while we passed someone who called out "yahowu," which is the same as "Hi, bud," in the States.

The Niha language sounds a lot like Hawaiian, full of glottals and vowels. It has a lot of v's and w's, so you get the impression of a "v-a-oo-v-u" when you hear a greeting. And a greeting is given without a smile, just a raised hand. Even when you do get a smile, the corners of the mouth are turned down. Jokes are told with faces like the mask of tragedy. We got pretty good at saying "Yahowu" with stern faces and turned down smiles and uplifted hands.

The path grew steeper. Pretty soon we were walking our bicycles and breathing hard.

We stopped to rest, and sat down on some stones.

"Look!" Bob said, "They're tooled." I looked. The stones were weatherworn, but they had been carved into low seats. I ran my hand over the warm stone. How old, I wondered.

We came to the house of the priest and the lay brother. They were expecting us. We delivered Father Johan's note and rested there for a while. The priest walked with us to the village above his church and wished us well.

The dirt path became a stone stairway. We left our bicycles and shouldered our baggage.

There are four courses of stairs in the path to Bawa Matalua, seven hundred stone steps in all. Have you ever tried to walk up seven hundred steps carrying two 16mm movie cameras, tripods and baggage besides? We had to stop at the top of each flight to rest. Up and up we went, until I couldn't go more than a few steps without stopping. My heart was beating so hard that I was sure everyone else could hear it. I was too tired to hold up my head. I saw just the stones under my feet and the next stones up. One more. One more.

Peter suggested that I give my camera to a small boy standing nearby. He assured me he knew this boy, and knew that he would be very careful.

Until that morning, I thought I would never let that Bolex out of my hand. I handed it to the boy. He bounded up those stairs like a mountain goat, the camera riding in his hand as easily as a cloud. I straightened my sun-hat, raised my eyes up at all the steps to go, took my courage firmly in hand, and started up again. One step, another…another…another. It seemed an eternity before Peter said, "There's Bawa Matalua."

High above us at the top of the stairs, two stone pillars stood silhouetted against the sky. Between the pillars were about a dozen ragged children. Half were clad in nothing but dirt, and the other half might as well have been. They disappeared when Bob produced his camera, but that bit of rest gave me just enough strength to get up those last long stairs.

The first thing we noticed after the children were the pigs and the flies. The pigs were eating the grass that grew up between the stones of the wide street. The flies were eating the pigs. These pigs looked more like wild boars than like domestic pigs. They lolled around as if they owned the place. I particularly remember one old female with her scrubby little brood rolling along beside her. She wore a complacent smile, and her belly was a self-satisfied tub.

With pigs ignoring us, and children trailing us, Bob and I stepped onto the remnants of a culture a thousand years older than Christianity.

Bawa Matalua is in the shape of a T. We entered on the left side of the crosspiece, and walked toward the center on a wide, stone-paved avenue between palm-thatched houses with high sloping roofs. At first, the place seemed deserted except for the children. Then we noticed silent people watching from the shadows. The street was wide as a courtyard and paved with cut stones. In front of each house were large, meticulously shaped stones. We knew from reading Loeb that the upright ones, the dolmans, were for male spirits and the horizontal slabs were for women.

At the top of the T was the chief's house.

The Bawa Matalua chief's house is more than twice as high as any of its neighbors. It has the same bulging front as the house on Pulau Teloh, and the same four great pillars and criss-crossed logs, but it is much bigger. Two immense, elaborately carved beams extend the entire length of the house and support its overhang. These beams curve up in front and in back, so that from the side, the house looks like a huge sedan chair.

At the front of the house, stand two tall dolmans, several smaller ones and some stone tables. In front of the dolmans, lie two highly polished "women's stones" where, according to the old religion, spirits live and people sit. These are about four by eight by three feet high, and carved with rosettes. The inner ends curve up like a kind of chaise lounge and are elaborately worked with more rosettes and little animals. Here was megalithic architecture at its highest, except for one clashing note. The roof of the house was a great sweep of rust-stained corrugated iron.

The village chief and his son were waiting for us at the chief's house. The chief's heavy-lidded eyes seemed never to leave our faces. His son was a heavy, taciturn man with a toad-like face. All the time we were in Bawa Matalua, we had a feeling that something was being hidden.

The entrance to the chief's house was essentially the same as the house at Pulau Teloh, except bigger. The main room was enormous. The atmosphere was different, too. People sat in the shadows, and children kept edging up behind the pillars. Whenever we looked around, there were dozens of them watching us with big, solemn eyes.

The chief asked what we wanted. We said that we would like to take pictures of their village and, if possible, their dances.

He studied us without blinking. Dance. Possible. But if we took the men away from their work, there would have to be a charge.

Of course. How much?

I hope we hid our dismay. The figure he gave was half as much as our budget for the entire trip! After fighting to get to Nias, we didn't have enough money left to buy what we'd come to get.

We explained our position to Mr. Begini and Peter.

They went into a long conversation with the chief and his son. All the time, the chief watched us with his heavy eyes.

I glanced out of the window. There was a man slaughtering a pig in the square. I asked if it would be all right for me to take a picture of him while the men talked. They nodded, and out I went.

The man stopped his work. I couldn't photograph him unless I paid him.

I didn't have any money on me. I don't know if I would have given it to him if I had. I went back upstairs. almost crying with vexation and anger. When I told the officials what had happened, they looked grim and got into a rapid discussion in Niha. I was advised not to go out alone again.

At last, the chief and his son decided they might provide a few dancers for a slightly smaller fortune. They'd have a meeting that night with the men of the village and discuss it.

It was time for lunch. We sat on the stone dais with Mr. Begini and Peter and shared our food. All they had was bread, but we had spreads and some Boston Brown bread, which they liked. They smiled more and started using another word, "bersama".

"Bersama" means "together." After we shared that meal, we were friends. We were a unit. We were bersama.

Mr. Begini asked whether we wanted to spend the night in Bawa Matalua or go back to the Richter's house. Neither of us wanted to face those steps again. But we were running out of money. How much would it cost to stay?

Peter said not to worry. He would take our IOU.

Mr. Begini vehemently objected. It wouldn't cost anything, he said. We were guests, weren't we?

Mr. Begini was wrong.

After lunch, Mr. Begini pointed out the stones where the chief and nobles used to sit. Someone was using them to dry laundry.

We saw the jumping stone. The jumping stone is about seven feet high, and built of cut stones into a flat-topped pyramid. A foot or so from its base, is a smaller stone from which the jumpers could get a start. In the old days, when a man had his first son, he had to jump over this stone with his baby in his arms to prove his prowess. If he didn't make it, of course, the baby died.

We could get a picture of somebody jumping over this stone for the price of a good hotel room in New York. I was beginning to think that the people of Bawa Matalua had spent the night plotting their profits.

Inside the balai were four stone pillars and four smaller stones, where the chief and the elders could sit and pass judgment.

Mr. Begini said that now the balai was used to store rice.

We knew it had once been a place to store heads.

Traditional Niha needed heads for all kinds of rituals. They put them under the foundations of their chief's houses. They used them to bless funerals and feasts. They offered them to sacred stones.

They got most of their heads in battles, which wasn't difficult because they were continuously at war. Heads were used in victory celebrations. Surplus heads were banked for future need. If they ran out of heads, they took one from a slave. They got slaves in war, or from debt. If someone owed property to the value of a slave, he or a member of his family might become a slave. The Niha traded in slaves. Old Portuguese trading records mention Nias as a source for slaves.

It started raining. We ran to the balai for shelter, and we had a theological discussion.

There was some confusion because of differences of languages, but the gist was something like this.

I gestured to a big dolman. "Did the old people honor that stone?"

"Yes," said Peter.

"No," said Mr. Begini.

Mr. Begini said that the old people didn't honor the actual stones. They honored the spirits in the stones.

Peter thought that might be right.

There was a discussion about whether a spirit was always in a stone, was imprisoned in the stone, or whether a spirit could leave its stone, wander around, and return to its stone, like coming home. Did some spirits have stones, and some not? Could more than one spirit live in one stone? Had the spirits always been in the stones, or had people put them there? Or had the gods?

If there were primal spirits in stones, there also had to be fresh spirits, because some people's spirits were put in stones and statues when they died. The street stones had such spirits.

Did all stones have spirits?

Mr. Begini closed the subject on a cheerful note. "It doesn't matter. We're Christians now. All the spirits are in heaven."

It stopped raining.

We left the balai and went into the breaking sunshine. I was aware of the stones beneath my feet. I was walking on ghosts.

Before dinner, we went to the baths.

I was the only woman in our party, so I was assigned a woman to accompany me. She spoke no Indonesian, so our communication was limited to smiles and signals.

The baths were at the far end of the street where we had entered in the morning. I followed my guide down steep stone steps to a place where the paths split. To our right was the way to the women's bath, to our left was the men's, and in the middle was a round stone table with carved hooks at the sides, where the chief could leave his clothes to signal that he was in residence.

My companion motioned me to the right. The stair was damp and covered with algae. I heard women's voices.

The bath was in a hollow. It was about twenty feet square, and lined with cut stones. About five feet above the floor, a shelf of rock extended out from the wall. The top was grooved with a V so that the water flowing into it was channeled to the two outer corners and fell into the pool below. The pool drained into a conduit that emptied through the wall on the other side. There were stepping stones under the surface of the water, and a ledge around the edge wide enough to walk on and to leave clothes. The place was filled with women bathing, washing clothes, and gossiping. Children with bamboo water carriers pushed along the ledge and reached over the heads of the bathers to catch the falling water.

As a guest, I was given the place of honor right under a spout, and my mentor gave me a demonstration of how to be modest though naked. One has to be clever with one's hands. As I was dressing, I was taken in hand by some schoolgirls whose Indonesian was about as good as mine. They led me up the steps, one hand on my arm, the other on their water carriers, saying "Don't fall, don't fall," and giggling.

They stayed with me by the chief's table while I waited for Bob. It was dark by then. Finally, we saw a flashlight bobbing its light along on the old stones and vegetation, and up came Bob with Peter and Mr. Begini. The girls ran on ahead of us all the way back to the chief's house, peering from around their bamboo water carriers and giggling.

The chief and the other officials joined us for a dinner of pig and rice. The parts of the pig that are reserved for guests and officials are the parts we use for giblet gravy.

The chief offered to tell us anything there was to know about the town, for about four times the cost of filming the slaughter of a pig.

We said, "Thanks, but no."

After dinner, we waited for the town council to decide about the dancing. They finally announced that they could present a small dance for a small fortune.

We were running short of money but after coming this far, we felt we had to get something. We said we would take their offer if they would have the dances in the morning or late afternoon when the light was good for filming.

They agreed. Everyone said goodnight, and we retired.

We slept on the big ironwood dais along the front of the house. The men rigged a privacy curtain for us that dropped to within about a foot and a half of the floor, so everybody could see in. I slept on the tiny mattress that we bought for the cameras, and Bob slept on a straw mat that Mr. Begini lent us. Moonlight seeped through the roof flaps. We lay looking up at massive beams and empty ritual shelves.

To one side hung a huge, beautifully carved drum, hollowed out of a log. The skin on the ends had rotted away, and the drum was filled with lumber and assorted junk. On one wall, a whole panel had rotted and been torn open to make a jagged peephole onto the square. Above us, draped a giant necklace of dusty pig's skulls.

"Do you feel like we're auditioning to be heads?" I whispered to Bob. He said he thought it wasn't proper to kill a guest in the chief's house.

We went to sleep with skulls watching us from above, and people watching us from the shadows. During the night, we were awakened by the weird cry of a kid bleating for its mother. Quite close. Either just below us, or in the same room. But we were tired. We slept well.

We breakfasted on rice and sauce, and went to the square to wait for our dancers. We saw Peter's boss, the District Officer, talking to the chief's son.

"I thought he'd turn up, "said Peter.

"Why," I asked. "Is he checking up on you?"

"No," said Peter, "But he likes to be sure that everything is under control. Some of these people are unpredictable."

The dancers weren't there yet.

By the time six men straggled in with work shorts showing under their costumes, the sun was almost directly overhead. We said that we couldn't take pictures until the light was better. So we drank tea until twelve thirty, when the District Officer told us that if we didn't take our pictures, the men would go back to work. They were dancing on their lunch hour!

We filmed in direct overhead sun. The dancers leaped around for about twenty minutes, then a fellow jumped over the jumping stone, and they all left.

Bob was furious, and I felt like crying. We'd spent all our time and money and effort and, yes, heart to get here, and it was all wasted! But what could we do?

We told Mr. Begini how we felt. He seemed at a loss as to what to say, but Peter, who had been uncharacteristically somber and detached during the whole miserable exhibition, seemed to have reached a decision. He drew Mr. Begini and the District Officer into a huddle. There was some animated discussion, then Peter removed himself and turned to us.

"There is another village you must visit," he announced.

We weren't sure that we were interested in another village.

But, said Peter, this village was different. It was his village, Helio Semintana. O.K.

The Bawa Matalua chief had been watching with narrowed eyes. Now he pushed forward.

Before we went to another village, he said, we could see the rest of his house.

For free?

A moment's pause. Then a curt nod. Was he feeling guilty? Or did he detect a threat to his prestige?

Behind the big room was another large room with carved pillars holding up the roof beams. Against a central wall, was a huge open hearth with a carved stone mantle. The hearth used to be used for cooking, but was now full of trash. In the next room, there were more carved pillars and another hearth backing up to the same wall and sharing a flue. This room had a little set of steps leading to a high peephole from which you could see down into the main room.

We saw the "chief's chair", a beautifully carved chest-shaped wooden platform. We saw a lot of chests. They all had large locks elaborately carved into their fronts. They don't open. They are memorials to a man's wealth.

At the end of a hall, two doors faced each other. One led to the chief's quarters, one to those of his wife. We saw the polished dais for sleeping, and a barred window under the high ceiling. The walls were hung with yellowing photographs. A few battered spears and some dusty artifacts hung on hooks along the wall. One was a yellow necklace. Our guide said that priestesses had worn necklaces like that, but they had been gold. This one was only beadwork. All the gold objects were sold long ago.

We saw the chief's wife's room, with its dark wood dais and high ceiling.

We stepped down into the cooking room, with big iron pots and utensils hanging around.

We saw no human or animal statues. No fetishes or spirit figures. We were reminded over and over that the Niha were Christian now, that the old statues had been sold or destroyed. We were told so often and so earnestly that I wondered.

We said goodbye to the huge, famous, shabby old house.

12

Helio Semintana

The steps back down were just as long as they had been on the way up. Tired and hot, we arrived at the priest's house where we stopped to rest.

Gosh, it was nice sitting in that little house, while the lay brother cooked doughnuts over a little kerosene burner, and we sipped cool tea. The priest offered to put us up for the night, and we almost took the offer, but Mr. Begini and Peter were adamant that we go on.

I hoped that our new accommodations wouldn't be another chief's house. Bob looked tired, and we were almost out of malaria prevention pills. Bob is a Malaria risk. He got the disease when he was on Okinawa, and sometimes he has relapses. But politics demanded that we accommodate our guides, so we shouldered our burdens, got on our bicycles, and started off again.

As we rode, Bob kept lagging behind. I told Peter to go ahead, that we would catch up, but he smiled his turned-down smile and said "bersama", and Mr. Begini bobbed agreement, so we all waited together. They were beginning to baby us, those two.

It took an hour to reach Helio Semintana and everything was glowing with that lovely golden color that comes just before sunset. The palm leaves waved in a soft evening breeze. The dirt of the path turned a luminous orange-brown. We breathed more easily as the air cooled and freshened.

Peter led us up a well-traveled road, with well-tended houses on each side and gardens of glorious tropical flowers. He proudly pointed out a school being built, and gestured to a large house a few yards down from the road. Down we went.

A graceful Niha girl invited us to sit on the porch. Her Indonesian was fluent and no wonder. She was the local schoolmistress. Her father was the Niha minister, and her brother was our companion, Peter. So Peter's father must be the local minister that Rev. Righter had told us about, the one who had kept the church going all through the war. So that's why Peter had been so eager! He was the preacher's kid. We were to be guests in his home! Bersama!

Peter introduced us to his little brother, Victor.

Victor was about five years old. He worshipped Peter, and had to accompany us wherever we went. Sometimes he was carried when his little legs couldn't keep up, but he was always there.

Victor had a big necklace of colored blocks, and a cap of many colors of which he was very proud. It was a kind of Tam O'Shanter made of eight gores, each of a different color. On top, was a little puff of a yarn ball that waggled when he walked. Whenever Victor was told to remove his cap, he'd first pull it way down until it rested on his ears and just missed his huge brown shiny eyes. Then he'd take it off. This showed you that he took it off because he chose to take it off, not because you had told him to.

When you imagine us walking around the village of Helio Semintana, you must include Victor, because he was always there.

After we got acquainted, Peter suggested that we go to see the village chief and ask if they would dance for us, here in Helio Semintana. "We dance better than they do in Bawa Matalua," he told us. We took his advice.

On the way to see the chief, we saw the polyclinic. It was a little cluster of buildings dating back to before the war. There were separate buildings for different purposes, and the whole thing was clean and full of bougainvillea bushes and banana trees. What a lot of work, I thought, was being done by only nurses and technicians!

The village chief welcomed us warmly, and because I was in our group, he asked his wife to join us. She offered us betel nut. She had a little serving set, a pouch with all the accessories.

First, she got out little squares of banana leaf. Then she cut up the betel nut and put a pinch of lime on top, then wrapped the whole thing in the banana leaf. This made a neat little package about the size of an unshelled peanut. She slipped these packages between her fingers, deftly holding them there until she had enough for everybody. She knelt and offered one to me first. I wanted to try it, but Bob said "No." I didn't want to shame him in front of our hosts, so I still don't know what betel tastes like.

We sat on the village chief's front porch, while everybody but Bob and I chewed betel, and discussed the unpleasant people of Bawa Matalua.

After a while, the head of the local dance society joined us. He and the village chief held their discussion in Indonesian instead of Niha so that we could understand. The dance man said he didn't think the villagers would dance for us unless we bought them a pig.

We said that we would never dream of asking them to dance for less, but that they would have to trust us for the money because we had barely enough to get home. The dance man agreed, and we gave him an IOU. That was one of the best investments we ever made.

We returned to Peter's father's home and had dinner on a long wooden table in the front room. I was the only woman. The rest of the women had eaten earlier. After dinner, we sat around chatting with our host. Peter's father was a patriarchal old gentleman with a true preacher's voice. When Bob told him I was a teacher at the Methodist school in Palembang, he wanted to know all about Methodist mission work. He said he might want to affiliate with the Methodist Church.

Wow! We had stumbled into something we didn't dare touch! Reverend Richter had bragged to us about his wonderful Niha minister, while his wonderful Niha minister was so upset about being replaced that he was looking for another church!

Next came prayers.

In the Lutheran Niha hymnbook, there are several simple tunes of about eight bars and a lot of scripture in Niha. The host reads a sentence of scripture, then everybody sings it.

The voices on Nias are the same as the voices on Pulau Teloh. Even the dogs didn't like them, and there were a lot of dogs. They listened respectfully when the old man read, but when everybody started that nasal singing, they threw back their ears, threw up their noses, and joined in. Bob got a coughing fit and had to hide his face in his handkerchief. I just choked and ducked. We tried to look devout, but it was an awful struggle.

After devotions, our host asked about American hymns. So we sang for them. They sang for us, and when we all knew the same song, we sang it together, each in their own language. Victor helped. Victor knew one song. It was the school song of the village school, to which he was not yet old enough to go, but he was boning up in advance. Every time we stopped singing, Victor's breathy little voice went on singing his own song.

That night, we slept on a proper mattress, with beautiful bed linen embroidered by the schoolmistress.

Next morning while we were eating breakfast, we saw a familiar figure climbing up the road. It was Doctor Thompson. With him were three nurses.

The schoolmistress ran out to meet him. They talked for a moment, then Dr. Thompson went off up the hill toward the polyclinic, and the schoolmistress came back. She was smiling.

Our car was here. Dr. Thompson had hitched a ride down. He hadn't been south for almost six months. He'd brought along two Niha nurses and a new nurse just out from Germany. He wanted to take back the secretary of the Helio Semintana clinic, and pick up two student nurses who needed further training. That is the way his nurse's training works, the schoolmistress said. First nursing school, then experience in the field, then more school, etc. until the nurses graduate and can be sent out to their permanent jobs.

Did we mind sharing our car?

I thought of all our baggage and all those people, but I was assured that there was plenty of room. This wasn't a regular jeep. It was an especially hardy land rover, with an extra large back end that could carry sixteen passengers. This turned out to be an exaggeration, but it sounded as though the vehicle could hold us all.

But what was Dr. Thompson doing, commandeering our transport? And now he expected us to take him and his whole entourage back! And he didn't even bother to ask us in person!

I fumed for a moment but couldn't think of an excuse to say "no," so I said "yes," and went back to tell Bob myself, so if he got upset he would take it out on me instead of the doctor. Bob wasn't feeling well, and was unlikely to welcome any changes.

Mr. Begini joined us for a walk through the town.

Like Bawa Matalua, Helio Semintana is on top of a hill, but it is a much smaller hill. The town is smaller, too, but all the houses are of the old type. Peter told us that it was illegal to build any other kind of house in the old compound. If you wanted another style, you had to go farther down the hill.

The village didn't have a chief's house. It had burned down, but the rest of the houses were in good repair. Although the people were obviously poor, they were clean. Here was a pride that had been missing at Bawa Matalua.

We walked over the old stones of the street, beside the old dolmans, and we admired the carvings in the paving stones. One had the snake and staff and head-dress of a priestess. One had a crocodile. One showed a man on horseback. One carving showed a carved pistol. The megalithic culture had survived long after the Niha were exposed to modern things. One stone on the way to Bawa Matalua had shown a tub-like old sailing ship, with a big cannon sticking out of it.

A new house had been built on the site where the chief's house used to be, but the chief himself had moved across the street. We went to the new house for our tea and cigarettes. It was not nearly as imposing as the Bawa Matalua house, but it shared many of the same features, and we felt more relaxed, perhaps because people smiled.

We noticed some complicated circular designs painted on the wall at the back of the house, and were told that these were done because the original ceremonial plates had been destroyed with the chief's house, and these took their symbolic place.

We passed through the village, and started down a path on the other side, into fields in the jungle. This was a burial ground for the old chiefs. One was Peter's ancestor. We were led to his grave. There, under a palm-thatched canopy, was a large raised concrete rectangle. On the front of it was a cross and what appeared to be a fetish animal. This fellow was taking no chances.

Peter pushed aside the tall grass to show us a long stone sarcophagus, open at the top. It looked a little like a boat.

We asked whether it was supposed to look like a boat, and were told no, it was just a sarcophagus. But when we looked it up later, we found that the word for casket, in Niha, is the same as for boat. We asked if it was open to accommodate temporary burial. Peter didn't know what we were talking about. But if they hadn't had temporary burial, where did they get all those ancestor's skulls that they had kept in the chief's houses? I didn't ask, but happily for our egos, we found out later that in the old days, a chief's body was left on a platform for a month or so before the bones were cleaned. How's that for amateur anthropology?

We left the cemetery and went back to have lunch, and wait for the dances to begin.

Our luck ran out. The sun went under a cloud and refused to reappear. It didn't rain, as we feared, but our pictures didn't turn out as brilliantly as we hoped, which was a shame because the dances were really something!

There were about thirty dancers, all in the old wardress we'd heard about: the metal or wood cape-like coats, the high hats or turbans, and kains tied around the waist, run between the legs, then let to drape in front. Some of the helmets were ornately decorated with cutouts of metal, and a few had metal moustaches draping in front. Each man carried a shield and a spear, except for one who wore only a loincloth.

First came an ominous procession of dancers, advancing toward us with leaping steps, shaking their shields and their spears in steady rhythm.

The watching children screamed and jumped back.

Someone had set up a piece of the trunk of a banana tree in the centre of the court. The top had been carved out to form a head-like knob, and the supple green bark had been stripped down on the sides to make a fringe like a cape. The dancers formed a circle around it, and began slow leaps. One, two, they shook their shields giving off a hollow rattle. Three, four, they hit their spears on their shields with a dead thudding sound. Their eyes were fixed on the thing in the centre, and their rhythm and their dance became faster and faster as they circled around and around. At the climax, the man in the loincloth dashed in, and with one sweep of his sword, decapitated the trunk, impaled it on the end of his spear, and waved it triumphantly while he ran down beside the dancers, who shouted and leaped in frenzied activity.

I almost knocked over the camera. Had we all forgotten it was only a banana tree?

Two by two, they danced out their prowess. Clash, clash, went the swords and spears as the warriors grimaced and shouted. Each belt held a ball of crocodile teeth that rattled as they leaped.

After each warrior had shown off, they all formed a line and paraded down the field, faces stern below those ornate helmets, spears held high and proud.

A man in ordinary clothes stepped in behind. The warriors turned, and the man fell down, faking terror and kicking his legs to the delight of the children who whooped with laughter. This was how the unfortunate banana tree had been taken in battle. This was mock ambush, very mock, and the comedy relief was needed. The man was captured and the ceremony continued.

Then came the last dance of all. The warriors circled and leaped as a big black boar that had been tethered at the side of the compound was brought into the circle. He squealed and struggled as if he knew what was going to happen. Poor boar! The village had belonged to him the day before. Now, thanks to us, he belonged to the village. He ran from place to place trying to break out of the circle of fearful warriors. The man who held his rope had to strain with all his might to hold him. Then, so quickly that it was only a flash, a warrior darted in and thrust his spear into the animal's neck. The bewildered boar slowly sank down and died, his red blood spilling on the old stones, while the warriors shouted and circled and leaped around him.

This was the end of the dances. Darkness was upon us, and we ran out of film. We were putting away our cameras, when Doctor Thompson came over with the new German nurse. Her name was sister Katrina, and she looked a little pale.

We told Dr, Thompson we were surprised to see him at the dances. He had so much work to do, and he must have seen the dances many times before.

He produced a half smile. "I thought I should be here," he said, "Sometimes someone gets overexcited." He started off, then turned back. "Be ready early tomorrow morning. There's a river we have to cross before dark." He strode off down the hill, his nurse beside him.

"Does that man run the earth?" Bob wanted to know.

We hoisted our equipment and went over to the balai to watch the boar being singed and quartered. Then we wandered down the hill to Peter's house. We bathed before supper. How lovely it feels to stand under the stars, with the smell of gardenias and sage, and soft spring water splashing over one's hot skin.

We ate dinner at the big wooden table in the front room. Mr. Begini joined us. The Bersamas were together again! After we finished eating, Mr. Begini asked how we liked our pig.

Bob and I exchanged startled glances. We had been eating the star of our show!

After dinner, we sat around the table and talked.

Where was Nias in the new world of an independent Indonesia?

It had problems.

The Niha weren't Moslem, and most government money went to Moslem areas. Poverty threatened, but to get money you had to have things to trade.

"We need something besides copra," said Mr. Begini. Everyone agreed, but no one knew what it might be.

We talked about the old people. We talked about families, and laws, and tribal history. We talked about the old religion.

We said we knew that the main god of old Nias had been Lowalingi, God of the Sky. But hadn't there also been a god of the earth and a god of the underworld? We couldn't remember their names.

"Oh," said Mr. Begini, "it was this way. There were the three main gods, Lowalingi, Jesu Keristi, and the Hantu Sutji."

We had prayers.

Jumping Stone

The Head

Pig skulls and empty thrones

Procession

Chief's
House

and

Warrior

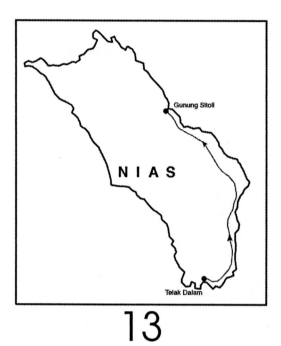

13

The Journey

Next morning, we were up bright and early. The land rover was already there, with full complement of driver and mechanic, and Mr. Begini, too, but breakfast wasn't ready. We remembered what the doctor had said about reaching a river before dark, but how hard could that be? It was only eighty miles. Or less. We decided to eat.

The schoolteacher was right. This land rover was different. The front looked like a regular jeep, but the back was like an open-sided delivery wagon. Along the sides were plank seats. We put all our stuff at the end nearest the driver, and I climbed in front with Bob and the driver, because Peter and Mr. Begini insisted on it. They climbed up in back,

Victor turned up wearing his cap, with his blocks all wrapped up in a bundle to take along with him to Palembang. We had to tell him he couldn't go with us.

Peter and Mr. Begini and I all assured him that when he was bigger, he could come to visit. I don't think he believed us. He had his little red cap pulled way down over his tear-stained face when we waved goodbye and bumped off.

Doctor Thompson, the nurses and the secretary were waiting for us at the foot of the polyclinic path. The doctor was in a black humor because we were late. He predicted all kinds of dire problems if we didn't get past that river before night-fall. Everybody climbed in, and we started off again.

Farther down the path, we stopped at the priest's house, where Doctor Thompson stayed in the jeep while Bob and I got out to say goodbye and thanks to the priest. Off we went again.

Did I tell you we were driving on a footpath? We didn't hit a road until we had jolted and rocked all the way to Reverend Richter's house.

Bob and I stopped to get the things we had left there, and to say goodbye and thank you.

The Richters offered us coffee, and even Doctor Thompson agreed to take a cup. Then he went off somewhere with the secretary and the new sister, and we were left with the Niha nurses, and the Richters.

We packed the land rover, and then packed it again better. Reverend Richter advised us to tie everything down, so we did.

We waited and waited, as the sun got hotter and hotter.

Finally Dr. Thompson reappeared. He'd just learned about the sister with the broken hip and was on his way to see her. He left the clerk and took a nurse.

So we sat some more. If we didn't make that river before nightfall, it wouldn't be because Bob and I stopped for breakfast.

Dr. Thompson reappeared with the news that the sister's hip was broken, and so was her leg in three places, and they all had been improperly set and would have to be broken again and re-set when the sister could be moved to hospital, which wouldn't be for at least another month. I thought of that hot little room and that great traction apparatus. Oh, dear!

Everybody climbed back into the land rover. We waved goodbye to the Richters, to Peter, and to dear little Mr. Begini who was smiling his widest turned-down smile. This time we really were off for Gunung Sitoli and home.

Betul, Pasti!

We started off on a gravel road, but it petered out quickly and we were wading through tiger grass and deep foliage. When we got out to stretch, we would lose sight of the land rover after a step or two.

Sometimes we broke out of jungle and skirted the sea, and I realized why everyone who has been on Nias mentions its beauty. The long low waves roll in like at Waikiki. The water is light blue, like the sky, and crystal clear. Sometimes there are rock formations out in the bays, high and carved into fantastic shapes. When the surf hits them, it breaks into glittering spray that leaps high into the air, before falling back into a myriad of snow-like bits of foam that ride the water back onto the rocks again.

Palms leaned like protective mothers over white beaches. Baby waves chased themselves over the sand.

We drove from sea to field to jungle. Every once in a while we passed a stone walkway to an old village. A couple of times, we stopped so Dr. Thompson could check on a clinic some place back in the jungle. Each time he assured us he would only be gone a couple of minutes, but he always took his whole staff, and they always took a long time, while Bob and the crew and I were left with the land-rover. We made friends with the kids who always materialize no matter how deep in the jungle you think you are.

We stopped at a lot of bridges. Most of them consisted of two big logs thrown across a crevasse, with split logs or sticks or rough boards laid across them. The crosspieces were just laid, not nailed down or anything. A lot of them had broken under the land rover on its way down. In several cases, we had to climb down into a gully to retrieve fallen lumber out of the streams that ran below.

Our usual system of crossing these rickety bridges was simple. The land rover stopped, and we all climbed out. We moved all the weight we could out of the land rover and carried it across by hand. Then we women waited on the far side, while the men arranged the cross pieces and joined us. Then the driver inched carefully across, keeping the land rover's wheels directly over the logs.

One bridge was burned out. The doctor had warned us of this. They had barely gotten across it on their way down. We stopped at the last bridge before it, and lifted a few logs to make a repair. The men tied a loop of rope around the logs, and tied the end to the truck. This didn't look like good physics to me. What was to keep the logs from slipping out?

They knew what they were doing. The clerk and the mechanic climbed up and rode the logs like water skis. Their weight retained the load.

The burned bridge was a mess! Somebody had taken shelter under it and used a piece of its wood to build a fire that had ignited the bridge itself. The land rover coming down hadn't helped. The bridge was caved-in completely on one side.

Our logs barely crossed the gap. Bob and Dr. Thompson had a long discussion with the driver and the mechanic. Then we gathered every piece of loose wood and bamboo that we could find, and the men rigged a platform that shook when we carried our baggage across. We moved to the side of the path to watch.

There wasn't much runway for a takeoff. The land rover gunned up as fast as it could and roared over. Its hind wheels barely touched our side before most of our new bridge slid gracefully down into the river behind us.

Bob and I gave up our front seats to the nurses and rode in back. One of the Niha nurses was sick, and Sister Katrina comforted her. The other Niha nurse had a crush on Doctor Thompson. She kept cuddling up to him in a proprietary fashion that the doctor bore stoically. Every time we came to another bridge, she would let out a little shriek and dive for his arm and look at him helplessly; he would pat her hand and extricate himself. Later on, he gave up and let her pretend to sleep on his shoulder.

Rain came and went. We inched along. "It might be faster walking," I suggested.

Dr. Thompson disagreed. "You can't walk it in less than three days," he said. He knew. He'd done it dozens of times.

Bridges were only built for gorges less than twenty feet across. For wider rivers, we just ploughed through. We would grind slowly down a path to the riverbank. The mechanic would get out and wade (in his clothes) out into the water. If he suddenly sank up to his shoulders, he'd back out of that spot and try another until he found a way that wasn't too deep for the bed of our land rover. Slowly, using the four-wheel drive, we'd slip and roar our way over the stones of the riverbed, and stop just off the far bank.

There was a rope tied around the front bumper. It was looped around so many times that I had thought it was a kind of ram to protect the car from shock if we hit anything. It turned out to be much more utilitarian than that. When we reached the far side of a river, people appeared from nowhere, the rope would be unwound and tied to our bumper, and our land rover would be hand-hauled up the riverbank. Some of these riverbanks were almost forty-five-degree angles of sticky mud and slimy stones. The land rover could get no traction at all. It took twenty or thirty barefooted, longhaired, Niha peasants, in ragged shorts, faded sarongs and scarves tied around their heads to hand-hoist us to dry land.

We learned to count in Niha,

"Sara, duo, ter-lu!" they'd chorus, and all pull on the "lu".

When we were safely on the path, our helpers all got a rupiah or maybe two. We'd raise our hands and call out "Yahowu!" and plough on into the jungle.

About three in the afternoon. we hit a real problem. We reached the river we had to cross before nightfall, and we could see the reason why. We were to be ferried across.

A big cable stretched between strong trees on either side. Attached to this cable was a pulley. The pulley was attached to the corners of a wooden raft, which, when we arrived, sat in the middle of the river being battered around on the current and collecting flotsam.

The system was beautifully simple. The pulley would keep the raft on course while it was being towed across the river. But the river was racing, and crossing would be dangerous, and it looked like the towrope had come loose from the raft. One end was tied to a tree on our side, but the other lay slack in the mud.

There were no natives in sight.

The mechanic wondered if there might be a shallow place we could ford. He waded in and got all wet for nothing. Dr. Thompson said the river was high because of the heavy rain in the mountains that day, and it should go down in an hour or so. We watched the water rise inch by inch. Large pieces of jungle began racing past.

The doctor and the nurses sat down on a log. The mechanic and the driver opened up the hood and began to fiddle with the engine of the land rover. They were having spark plug trouble, so with Bob's help they took out the plugs and cleaned them thoroughly. The engine still missed, so Bob showed them how to use a coin to set the proper gap for the spark. Then they contemplated the wiring.

Someone suggested we eat. Bob and I still had a couple of cans, and the driver offered us part of his meal. The hospital people didn't have much, so we opened some stew and heated it up on the engine. We ate. Then the hospital people returned to their log; the driver, the mechanic, and Bob returned to their tinkering, and I watched the river.

It seemed to be leveling off.

People began gathering on both shores. Someone called across. "Thompson?"

"Eeyah!"

There was an old gray outrigger hull pulled up on our side of the river. A couple of men pushed it upright, produced a paddle and pulled out the loose end of the towrope. They pushed off and, staying as close as they could to our somewhat sheltered bank, they paddled upstream. Then they headed mid-stream and, by dint of much frantic paddling against the current, managed to be swept only a few yards past the landing on the other side. One man waded in through the mud and tied his end of the rope to a tree, while the other waded out and started to work his way along the rope toward the raft.

While this was going on, a new man appeared on the other side and began screaming across to us. Our driver began shouting back. This conversation went on for quite a while, and all that time the poor fellow in the river was clinging to the rope, while his head went back and forth like a spectator at a tennis match. Finally, I guess he got tired of being buffeted about by the current. He struggled the rest of the way to the raft and pulled himself, dripping, aboard.

You'd think our problem was solved. Not so. We were in a jurisdictional dispute. The fellow across the river claimed that the ferry was his personal business, and our driver had broken the law by using men who had no right to touch his ferry or pull his rope.

Our driver called back that the ferry was his business, because his boss ran the road concession. Both men were so mad that it was lucky the river was between them. The fellow on the raft put his arms behind his head and appeared to go to sleep, while Doctor Thompson was doubled up with laughter.

Doctor Thompson translated part of the conversation.

"Only the government tells me what to do!"

"The government is the people! I am the government!"

Eventually, the argument wore out; we pulled the ferry over to our side, and the fun really started.

The men dragged a couple of planks out of the underbrush, laid them across the mud to the ferry and, with much threatening creaking of lumber, the land-rover crept onto the raft. So did several people from the neighborhood.

There was a lot of "sara, dua, ter-lu"ing until we got to the middle of the river, when somebody called out and everything stopped. A man was shouting and pointing up to where the pulley was silhouetted against the sky.

We looked up. The cable was almost frayed through!

We stayed in the middle of the river for about twenty minutes while they talked this over.

Finally, the "Sara, duo, terlu"-ing began again, and we eventually arrived on the other side. But the towrope had been tied wrong, so we arrived about four or five feet downstream from where we should have been. Across the mud from us lay solid jungle.

What to do?

Everybody had an idea and they were all different.

At last a rope was run up on shore and secured around a stump. Everybody "Sara, duo, terlued" at a great rate, but the rope was attached to the wrong corner so it didn't help. The stump was rotten and gave way, dumping the men all over the ground.

Doctor Thompson and Bob climbed off the raft and waded through the mud to where some other men were attempting, with much argument, to lash the rope around a little sapling no larger than my wrist. Under Bob's supervision, a guide line was strung around one tree while another line went around another tree, and a system was set up whereby three men held the guide rope and secured the slack while everybody else "Sara, duo, terlu"ed and pulled.

It worked pretty well. We were almost where we wanted to go, when another dispute broke out because some of the men weren't pulling on "lu" and expected to get their rupiahs for work that others were doing.

Two of the men holding the guide rope left to join in the fight, and the third went to sleep, so we swung back to where we'd been in the first place.

Bob and Doctor Thompson tried to restart the system again, but nobody would listen because they'd tried our way and it hadn't worked.

It was twilight, so we held flashlights while they wove webs of rope around trees, exerted huge amounts of energy, and perspired buckets until, about an hour and a half later, they managed to drag the land-rover from the raft to the planks in the mud where it was hauled valiantly up the bank by about a third of the original force. The rest had gone home.

"Yahowu," We struggled off into pitch-black jungle.

"At least we got across the river before nightfall," said Bob.

The next few hours, we alternately sang and slept.

We were almost to the last big river, when the land rover let out a dreadful grinding and clattering and clanking and stopped.

Everybody got out except Dr. Thompson who was asleep.

Bob and the mechanic crawled under the car and reappeared with the news that there was a tooth broken on the rear differential. Bob suggested they disconnect it. After all, the land rover was a four-wheel drive vehicle. The driver looked at Bob as if he were crazy, but he let him operate. Off we went on front wheel drive.

About this time, Doctor Thompson woke up and told us that there was a house not too far away that had a phone. We could call the hospital at Gunung Sitoli, and they would send down the hospital car.

Cheered by this thought, we ground on until our land rover locked up and stalled again. We walked to the village.

The village had a phone because the village chief was an important man on Nias. He had a great big house with several other buildings, including a clinic, nearby. He came out in his sleeping sarong to give us coffee and fruit, while Doctor Thompson went to use the phone. He tried and tried, but never got his call through. It was well after midnight when he gave up. We thanked our host and went back to the land rover.

Bob came to the rescue again. He and the mechanic took out the entire rear drive shaft. For the rest of our trip, we used front wheel drive while the rear drive shaft clanked around under our feet, and the driver muttered about the crook that had charged him for big parts that he obviously didn't need.

Meanwhile Bob and I worried about our ship. Would we get there on time? Bob had never gotten a reply to his cable. He had said we could be reached on the Celia's short wave, but that was before the Captain told us he had no use for Indonesian shipping news, so he never turned his radio on.

We were running out of money. No one knew where we were. What would we do if we missed the ship?

"Speaking of money," Dr. Thompson had been eves dropping, "I renegotiated your contract for this car?"

"You what!"

"Yes. He was cheating you."

Dr. Thomson had cut two thirds off the cost of our trip.

The land rover slowed and stopped. We had reached our last river. It was an exceptionally wide river, and it was high.

The mechanic climbed out into the chilly night breeze and waded into the water with his clothes on. He waded back out again, shaking his head.

The river wasn't deep, but it was fast. We could see that in the moonlight.

The mechanic, trembling in his wet clothes, went off to find people who might push us across the river and pull us up when we got to the other side. He came back with two sarong-clad farmers stumbling along behind him, blinking sleep out of their eyes. They, too, waded into the river and came out shaking their heads. Bob said we might have made it if we still had both drives, but the front wheel drive wasn't powerful enough. We had to wait for the river to go down.

The damp chill of a tropical night goes right to your bones. We pulled out everything we had that might keep people warm. We covered the nurses with our sweaters. We wrapped our blanket around the clerk. We dragged out Bob's last shirt, a heavy maroon camping shirt, and put it around the shivering shoulders of the mechanic. The two farmers rigged a flimsy shelter-half out of a sarong and disappeared inside. Bob and I huddled under our raincoats to cut the chill night wind, while a great cold moon touched the scene with snowy white light. Bob fell into uneasy sleep.

I couldn't sleep. I slid out from under our raincoats and went to watch the river. I heard Dr. Thompson before I saw him.

"Your husband has malaria," he said.

"He got it during the war. It recurs. We've run out of preventative."

He pushed a paper packet into my hand. "Take these."

'Thanks, but we'll be home in two days."

"Take them." It was that irritating, commanding voice.

"Thank you."

We sat and watched the river for a while.

"There's a lot of malaria here," he said, "and dysentery, and yaws, and rickets." He was talking half to me and half to the river. Malaria could be treated, he said, and dysentery could be avoided with proper hygiene, but the thing that bothered him most was vitamin deficiency, because it was so preventable. "The Niha say fresh vegetables are for animals. They won't eat them, even when they can get them. We try to get them to eat the tops of the taro. They don't like the taste."

"I thought they'd do anything you wanted them to," I said. Did he detect my sarcasm?

He chuckled. "Like at the river?"

"They were trying to protect you. They admire you. They almost worship you."

He paused for a moment. Then he said, "That's a problem. The people say they are Christian, but their old animism is still strong. A lot of them believe in sympathetic magic. They think that because I'm a doctor, all they have to do is touch me or stand in my shadow and they'll get well. Some do, of course, and that makes it worse. Sometimes, if I give a prescription to be filled at the clinic pharmacy, they eat it instead, or tear it up into water and drink it."

"Must be hard."

"Sometimes."

We watched the water for a while.

Then, "Some anthropologists came through here before the war. They studied South Nias. The people showed them everything they had. The anthropologists had a lot of money, and they bought everything they saw. After they left, the people celebrated their good fortune until everything was gone. Now there are Niha treasures scattered around the museums of the world, and there's nothing left for the Niha."

He stood up.

"When I first met you, I thought you were tourists. Then I was afraid you were anthropologists…You should get some sleep."

A couple of hours later, Bob woke, cramped and chilled, and climbed over the rest of us to go out and look at the river. It was down. He woke the driver, who yawned, stretched, and went down to look, too. One by one, the rest of our party woke and straightened our aching limbs. The farmers crawled out from under their sarong. Slowly our caravan came to life and pretty soon our crippled vehicle crept toward the water that, although it still rushed along, had dropped a couple of feet.

We inched our way across, the mechanic and the two farmers wading by our side, pushing and holding the land rover when it slipped in the fast current. A couple of times, the wheels slipped and the swirling black water rose just even with the bed of the truck. But we made it.

Close to the other side, we stopped on a stone pebbled island while the mechanic waded the rest of the way and roused more farmers to pull us up on the other side.

On we went.

The footpath gave way to a narrow dirt road. We caught sight of the sea again. The horizon was lightening with coming dawn.

The sun peered over the tops of the trees when we pulled into the outskirts of Gunung Sitoli. We stopped for some strong hot tea at a roadside shack. Farmer's carts passed us on their way to market, and we could hear chickens waking up. The chill night wind gave way to the warmth of morning. It was day when we rolled into Gunung Sitoli and climbed off the land rover at the rest house.

It had taken us twenty-two hours to go less than eighty miles.

The Journey

Church at Telak Dalam

On the Way

Waiting by the River

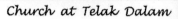

Pat   Bob

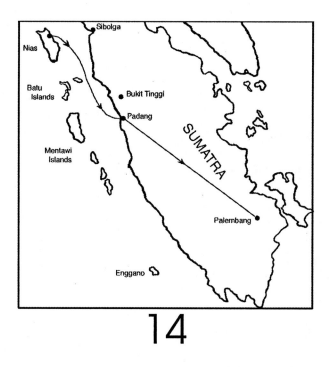

14

Home

The KPM ship wasn't in yet.

Dr. Thompson offered to turn in the land rover on his way to the hospital. Bob objected, pointing out the drive lying in the back, but Dr. Thompson said he would take care of it and Bob should go to bed. So we unloaded our things, gave Dr. Thompson money for the land rover, and waved goodbye.

We ate breakfast on the rest house verandah, then went to our room and climbed into bed. We didn't get up again until afternoon.

Except once.

I was awakened by a ship's whistle. Was it the KPM ship? I went out to see. There was a vessel on the horizon, its smoke black against the sky. I watched it come nearer, and the nearer it came, the more familiar it looked. It was the Celia. I went back to bed.

That night, Bob got the shakes. I put a hand on his burning forehead, gave him one of Dr. Thompson's pills, and suggested the hospital, but he would have none of it. He stuttered that he'd get over it himself.

The next day I learned how limited Nias's resources really are.

I needed fruit for Bob. There was no pineapple, no papaya, no mango, and the bananas were all too green. I wandered all over town, the market, street stalls, and shops, everywhere. I finally located a couple of rather hard limes, a little bread, some cookies, a can of condensed milk, and a can of sardines in tomato sauce. I also found a can of grapes. Have you ever had canned grapes? Believe me, they're delicious when you haven't seen fruit for days!

Bob had bread and hot limejuice for breakfast.

At noon, I took our little pail to the restaurant to see what I could get. I didn't want to give Bob spicy sauces when he was so sick, so I bought some rice. We ate it with sardines as sauce. I had grapes for dessert, and Bob drank tea until he couldn't drink any more. That afternoon, he was sleeping easily and his skin was cool.

We met nice people while we waited for our ship to come in.

The manager of the rest house was an old man who had worked for the Dutch. He was very polite and very servile. He had a mynah bird that spoke only in Indonesian. It could say, "Good morning, sir," and "Good evening sir." and "Freedom!"

We met the new head of the Nias secondary schools. He had completed one year at Gaja Mada University, then dropped out to get a job. His small, smiling wife was always nearby, cooking, washing, or just sitting on the steps and talking. She had been a student, too. They had left school so they could afford to get married.

We met the new Assistant District Officer who had us to his house for tea. He was from Aceh, and wasn't happy in Gunung Sitoli. His wife had been sick with malaria ever since they came, his older son didn't like the school, and his younger son was frail. We clucked our sympathy. The Acehnese are famous for not getting along with anybody but other Acehnese.

We had dinner with our old friend, the Information Officer. He wouldn't take our IOU for the broken battery. He said it was old, and he had requisitioned another. His wife and little boy had just arrived from Medan because family housing on Nias had only recently become available. Their house was small and roughly finished, but he loved it.

He had only gone through the fifth grade, but he observed a great deal and thought about a lot of things.

He thought it would be a good idea to keep offices open in the evening instead of during the midday heat, because thinking would be easier.

He had figured out that America must have independent voters. "You have two parties. If everybody belonged to a party, your elections would always turn out the same way, and there would be no need to have them. So you must have many people who don't belong to any party, and that is why you have campaigns."

In his opinion, there are three factions in Indonesia. One is made up of people who would rather be under a colonial system, so they don't have to think. The second includes people who are out to get everything for themselves. The third consists of patriots like himself who want a strong, free Indonesia.

He said that things go wrong when the first two factions work together against the third, because nothing gets done.

He said that it would take at least twenty years for Indonesia to be able to stand as a really strong government. He put his arms around his little boy and said, "I won't do it, he will."

He walked with us down to the dock where we got into a conversation with some coolies loading a lighter. One of the coolies said that the trouble was that the Dutch hadn't built enough schools. "They made us stupid."

Our host lost his temper. "No one can make you stupid," he said. "Can you think?"

"Yes," said the coolie.

"Then you're not stupid. Maybe you haven't had schooling, but nobody can make you stupid. You do that for yourself."

The next day we ran into some of the agent's men off the Celia. They had abandoned the ship, and were going to Sibolga on the government boat rather than spend another hour with the Captain. They planned to ask the chartering service in Medan if they could break their charter and hire another ship. Good business depends on good relationships, they said, and the Captain wasn't helping. We wished them well.

Police quarters were in a long barracks-like building across the street from the rest house. There was a big can hanging beside the front door. Every hour a man came out and beat on the can so everybody would know what time it was.

Behind the police quarters was a playing field, and beyond that, the beach. We wandered down to watch the sunset. It was glorious! The sky looked as if it had been slathered with a rainbow.

A puppy was guarding the waters edge. Every time a wave rolled in, he barked like mad, and when it receded, he chased it. He was doing his job very well, but time comes for even puppies to knock off work and go home to bed. He trotted off when the next wave washed over my sandals.

We watched the moon come up, big as a merry-go-round. The evening mists came in. A little outrigger slipped through the haze on its way to the harbor. Palms waved against the sky. We went back to the rest house and drifted into sleep, while somewhere in the distance someone played a harmonica. The regular soft rush of the surf soothed our dreams.

We were wakened by the sound of a ship's whistle.

We dressed and ran out to see. In the harbor rode the biggest ship I have ever seen in my life! The KPM Kasimbar had arrived!

It had cabins!

It had a covered deck!

It was a monster!

I will never understand how it shrank so much between Gunung Sitoli and Padang.

We spent the morning packing and saying goodbye to everyone. Then, at two-thirty, we entered our floating palace, stowed our gear in our stateroom, and stood on the deck watching the Kasimbar unloading lumber. A little chug-chug of a boat came alongside with a bunch of coolies. The giant boom of the Kasimbar lifted logs off the deck and swung them into the water. The coolies jumped onto the logs and, twirling them and riding them like lumberjacks, tied them into a raft. Sometimes someone fell into the water. Sometimes someone jumped in and swam around with his clothes on just for fun. When a raft was big enough, the little chug-chug would tow it back to shore and come out again for more. Lighters filled with copra hovered around, waiting to replace the lumber in the Kasimbar's holds.

Loading was finished by nightfall. The deck vibrated under our feet. Moonlight glistened on the Kasimbar's wake as Bob and I watched Nias disappear below the horizon.

Our crossing to Padang was uneventful. We were the only occidentals on board, so we ate with the Captain. With silverware! On real China! There were about 50 Chinese and Indonesian cabin passengers aboard, 245 deck passengers, and 70 pigs trussed up in baskets and piled on top of each other on deck. This doesn't count the baby pig that someone gave the Captain's little girl. There were five monkeys, several parrots, and a lot of rubber. During our 30 hours on board, two people died and one was born. We didn't see them. Our biggest challenge was how to be presentable at the Captain's table.

You would think that our troubles would be over when we got to Padang, but again we had no place to stay. While we were dawdling with our goodbyes on the Kasimbar, a ship came in from Djakarta and booked all the hotel rooms.

We sat in the lobby of the Muara Hotel while Mother Hubbard called all over Padang, including, at our suggestion, the Chinese hotels. No luck.

So she gave us her guest room. She lived behind the hotel in a sprawling bougainvillea draped cottage. There were clothes in the closet. Someone had doubled up. How nice can you get?

We slept wonderfully!

Next morning, we faced another problem. How to get back to Palembang? Our reservations had been for the week before.

Mother Hubbard saved us again. She introduced us to The Garuda Airlines manager who lived in the Muara Hotel, and we were on the next plane.

It's three hundred miles from Padang to Palembang, and it passed in a wink.

The company hostess came running out in great excitement. Where'd we been? She'd been meeting every plane for a week!

Our cable had never left the office!

We crossed the river in a sampan with our baggage piled up beside us. As we neared the landing, three company wives tripped down the dock, tailored dresses sparkling, white pumps spotless, chattering like birds as they boarded the company launch.

I had the same feeling I had when we opened our last can of food beside that river on Nias. "Well, this is it!"

A lot of people said they were happy to see us. One of the women gushed that she was dying to travel the way we did. We warned her that there were discomforts, but she laughed them off. She was an old timer. She could rough it. She had spent two whole nights at the Muara Hotel in Padang!

Happiest of all was Hamlet Ape, who swung, squeaking, off the roof and bit us all over to make sure we were all right, then snuggled down in my arms, his long gibbon arms around my neck, and refused to let go.

I guess that's about it.

Love,

Pat

Epilogue

What happened then? What happened to the injured nun and Dr. Thompson's clinics? Did Victor ever get to Palembang? A story is supposed to have a beginning, a middle and an end. How did this end?

I don't know. This isn't a story. It is only a segment of a much longer journey, and it's been fifty years. We paid for our pig. All I have left is a faded film, a beautiful seashell, and the carbon of a long letter.

The world has changed a lot, but Indonesia still faces vast problems, economic, ethnic, religious and political. Now an earthquake and a tsunami have devastated most of the west coast of Sumatra.

What happened to Nias in all this? What happens to an island when the earth moves?

Not what you'd expect. Nias is being saved by the sea.

A few years back, someone found out that the surf off South Nias is some of the best in the world. Surfers began coming from all over! You can get a boat directly from Padang to Telak Dalam. You can fly from Sibolga to Gunung Sitoli, and from Gunung Sitoli, it's only an hour to Telak Dalam. You can take a day tour. You can see tribal dances at Bawa Matalua and sleep in a hotel that night.

When earthquakes shook Nias, surfers from all over the world took notice and help is coming from all over the world.

Tolong Menolong.

Glossary of Indonesian Words and Terms

adat: - tradition, a set of customs, attitudes and beliefs that is unique to a culture

bahasa, Bahasa: - a general word for language; the capitalized form is used as an abbreviation for Bahasa Indonesia, the official Indonesian language

balai: - a pavilion, a town center, sometimes a storeroom, sometimes a sanctuary

begini: - like this

benar: - true, genuine

betel: - a nut with analgesic properties that, when chewed, turns the mouth bright red and the teeth black

betul: - true, correct

bersama: - together

eeyah: - yes (as used in south Nias)

gamelan: - a set of traditional musical instruments

garuda: - a gigantic mythical bird, a Hindu diety

Hantu Sutji: - Holy Ghost

Isu Keristen: - Jesus Christ

juga: - also

kain: - a long cloth worn by women

kami: - we, excluding the person addressed

kita: - we, including the person addressed

Keristen: - Christian

lekas marah   - quick to anger, a bad character trait

Lowalingi: - Niha god of the heavens

nasi:	- cooked rice
nasi tim:	- overcooked rice
pasti:	- true, certain, definite
patut:	- proper, polite
rupiah:	- Indonesian currency. In 1956, the exchange rate was $1.00 = 11.40 rupiahs. In 2005, the rate was about $1.00 = 10,000 rupiahs.
sara, duo, ter-lu:	- one, two, three (in Niha)
sarong:	- a tubular cloth worn by men
selop:	- slipper
tolong:	- to help
menolong:	- to receive help
tolong menolong:	- to help each other
yahowu:	- hello (in Niha)

Glossary of People and Places

Aceh (Atjeh):   - the westernmost province of Sumatra

Acehnese: - the people of Aceh; their characteristic physical features

Assam: - an Indian region in the Himalayan foothills, just below Bhutan

Batak: - the major group of people in North Sumatra, adjacent to Aceh; significantly different in appearance from Acehnese

Batu Islands: - an island group just southeast of Nias

Bawa Matalua: - a village in south Nias historically noted for its megalithic culture

Bukit Tinggi: - a hill station in west central Sumatra

Bupati: - the highest government officer on Nias

Chamat: - the highest government officer on Pulau Teloh

Djakarta: - the largest city and capital of Indonesia, on the northwest coast of Java

Enggano: - a primitive island near the southeastern tip of Sumatra

Gaja Mada University: - a prestigious university in Bandung, Java

Gunung Sitoli: - the largest town and capital of Nias

Helio Semintana: - a village in south Nias also noted for its megalithic culture; (Recent spelling is Hilismaetano.)

Java: - a major island of Indonesia, between Sumatra and Bali

Jogjakarta: - a city and former sultanate in Java

Minangkabau: - the major group of people in central Sumatra, adjacent to the Batak

Nias:	- an island off the coast of northwestern Sumatra, Indonesia,
	   Home of an ancient megalithic culture,
	   More recently noted for its great surf,
	   Most recently known for proximity to the seismic disturbance that
	      caused the great 2005 tsunami, and for powerful after-shocks that
	      killed hundreds of its people.

Niha:	- the people of Nias; the language of Nias
Padang:	- a trading port and the capital of West Sumatra
Padang Sidempuan:	- a minor town southeast of Sibolga
Palembang:	- the capital of South Sumatra; a major city and deep-water river port
Pulau Teloh:	- a town in the Batu Islands
Ranau:	- a lake and area in southern Sumatra
Sibolga:	- a trading port in western Sumatra, just opposite the island of Nias
Sumatra:	- a major island of Indonesia, over 1,000 miles long, 250 miles wide; The sixth largest island in the world and third largest in Indonesia
Tapanuli:	-a former province on western coast of Sumatra
Telak Dalam:	-a trading port at the southern end of Nias